Ancient Civilizations

A Complete Overview on The Incas History, The Byzantine Empire, Maya History & Maya Mythology

Eric Brown

© Copyright 2018 by Eric Brown

All rights reserved.

The following eBook is reproduced below with the goal of providing information that is as accurate and reliable as possible. Regardless, purchasing this eBook can be seen as consent to the fact that both the publisher and the author of this book are in no way experts on the topics discussed within and that any recommendations or suggestions that are made herein are for entertainment purposes only. Professionals should be consulted as needed prior to undertaking any of the action endorsed herein.

This declaration is deemed fair and valid by both the American Bar Association and the Committee of Publishers Association and is legally binding throughout the United States.

Furthermore, the transmission, duplication or reproduction of any of the following work including specific information will be considered an illegal act irrespective of if it is done electronically or in print. This extends to creating a secondary or tertiary copy of the work or a recorded copy and is only allowed with an expressed written consent from the Publisher. All additional rights reserved.

The information in the following pages is broadly considered to be a truthful and accurate account of facts, and as such any inattention, use or misuse of the information in question by the reader will render any resulting actions solely under their purview. There are no scenarios in which the publisher or the original author of this work can be in any fashion deemed liable for any hardship or damages that may befall them after undertaking information described herein.

Additionally, the information in the following pages is intended only for informational purposes and should thus be thought of as universal. As befitting its nature, it is presented without assurance regarding its prolonged validity or interim quality. Trademarks that are mentioned are done without written consent and can in no way be considered an endorsement from the trademark holder.

Incas

A Comprehensive Look at the Largest Empire in the Americas

Table of Contents

Introduction 7
Chapter 1: Seeds of an Empire 9
Chapter 2: A Difficult Place to Live 17
Chapter 3: A Day in the Life 23
Chapter 4: The Gods 36
Chapter 5: Decline and Downfall 47
Chapter 6: Remains of the Day 56
Conclusion 62

Introduction

When the conversation begins about the great civilizations of the Americas, there are three general that come to mind: the Mayans, the Aztecs, and the Incas. But while the Mayans and the Aztecs were similar in their cultures and geographically very close together, the Inca Empire was separate both by land and social structure. Because of these assumptions made, much of what is 'known' about the Inca Empire is actually misattributed from these perceived connections.

The Inca Empire covered the Andes mountain range in South America, covering today what is Peru and Chile. They flourished for over 200 years, quickly becoming the largest and most powerful region in the Americas before their potential was tragically cut short by the invading Spaniards. Today, not much remains of the great Inca but ruins of their cities and whispers of their legacy.

Or, is there? After all, just because your high school history class never talked about it, doesn't mean the information isn't out there. In fact, we have more knowledge pertaining to the Inca Empire than we do on either the Mayans or the Aztecs, perhaps even combined.

In the following pages, you will learn all you need to know to shock friends and family with your knowledge of Inca culture and history. From the foundations of their empire to their impractical geological location, and how they managed to flourish despite the odds. Customs and social structure, government and politics, and the lives of citizens. Religion and warfare. Everything culminating with the Inca's downfall at the hands of Columbus and his disease-ridden, death-mongering conquerors.

In fact, by the time you've finished this book, you may be ready to school your teachers.

Chapter 1: Seeds of an Empire

The Inca Empire did not actually form until sometime in the 1200s, making it younger than the University of Oxford. However, this does not mean that the area was uninhabited or entirely primitive. The indigenous people of the Andes mountain range lived for thousands of years prior to this, untouched and undisturbed.

Scholars referred to these people as 'pristine,' meaning they were untouched by any neighboring indigenous people. The Andeans developed their own languages and ways of communication. The primary language used was Quechua, which would later go on to be the official language of the Incan Empire. Notably, the Andeans had no written language. Nor were they an oral society, like most other American indigenous groups. Instead, information was conveyed through something called the 'quipu,' a series of intricately knotted and color-coded strings. Fascinating though they are, there are few left in existence, and no one has ever been able to decipher a quipu. Whatever information is recorded in those strings, we will likely never know.

Andean people are also notable for never developing the wheel. The rocky, uneven terrain of their homeland makes this development understandable, however, as a wheel could prove anything from a hindrance to useless. Instead, Andeans used llamas as pack animals, and before the empire, they rarely traveled.

An impact the Andean civilizations had that lasted through the Incan Empire was their lack of currency. Instead, they existed on a system of reciprocity, distributing goods and services in exchange for labor.

The Tiwanaku

In Bolivia, where the city-state of Tiwanaku was situated, a civilization lasted hundreds of years and predated the Incas by almost two centuries. Ranging from about 300-1150 CE, they expanded their reach through politics and trade, but their downfall came at the hands of climate change, as was so often the case in such an area.

The Wari

Neighbors of the Tiwanaku, the Wari civilization formed around 600 BCE. A wealthy people, with its own administrative structure, they co-existed peacefully with the Tiwanaku for centuries. The Wari civilization lasted until the same climate change caused their crops to fail, and their power structures began to crumble. In the time that passed after those two small empires saw their fall, a new power was beginning to grow.

Kingdom of Cusco

The semi-legendary figure of Manco Capac began life as a nomad, a wanderer of the mountains. With his small tribe, he found the Huatanay valley high in the Andes. The area was only mildly settled by other small tribes, and so Manco Capac settled his family and turned the area into the city we know as Cusco.

Because of the lack of written records, it's hard to know just what of Manco Capac's life was real and what was a mere myth. Legend says he founded the city of Cusco itself, but history shows us that the valley was already well occupied and the city was a small but thriving area. How much Manco Capac did to found Cusco doesn't matter so much as what he did afterward, however, as it was under his leadership that the city turned from a mere settlement into a kingdom. He abolished the local practice of human sacrifice, and set new laws and administration in place. The city expanded, new buildings included a stone palace where he and his family lived.

In the native language of the Incas, Quechua, the kingdom was named 'Qosco.' This makes it notable among Spanish-conquered cities for having retained its native name, and not be given a new, Catholic name. 'Qosco' in Quechua means 'center.' This name would mark its importance as the center of the future Inca Empire.

Manco Capac reigned for forty years and died peacefully. His son, Sinchi Ruq'a, took up the mantle after him, establishing a dynasty that would last for generations. Leaders of the Kingdom of Cusco would take the title 'Sapa Inca.' The ninth of these men, a great visionary named Pachacuti, would expand the kingdom even further.

Pachacuti was not born with this name, it was given to him to describe his great deeds. Born as Cusi Yupanqui, he was a younger brother and not even meant to inherit the title of Sapa Inca. But when he was a young man, Cusco fell under siege to a neighboring tribe, the Chankas. While his father and brother fled, Cusi Yupanqui faced his enemies head-on. He fought so fiercely, those who witnessed the battle said even the stones raised themselves from their sleep to fight alongside him. It was because of this event that he was given the new name Pachacuti, which means 'Earth Shaker.' He was named Sapa Inca, for his true loyalty to Cusco had shone while his cowardly family hid away.

But Pachacuti was not content to remain. He expanded Cusco in all directions, bringing all surrounding tribes under his rule. By his death, the Kingdom of Cusco was twice the size of what it had been. In the twenty years of his son's reign, it had doubled again. It is during this frame of time that the Kingdom of Cusco became what we know today as the Inca Empire, and it would only continue to grow and expand.

The Four Nations
The Incan Empire, during the height of its glory, was divided into four sub-kingdoms, like territories. Each of these quarters was grouped due to the previous tribes that had existed and had control of the land, before the Incan expansion. The Incas, a little like the Romans, chose to absorb rather than conquer.

Each of these territories was given the suffix –suyu, which in Quechua means 'region.' The prefix of their name was usually attributed to the direction of the province, and the Quechua names for the natives living in that area. Government administration meant that these regions still maintained a level of autonomy within the empire.

Chinchasuyu was the northernmost province. The name comes from the Chincha culture, a trader kingdom that occupied the area. 'Chincha' is also a word that, in Quechua, means 'north,' denoting the direction. The region stretches into the Peruvian deserts and was one of the larger quarters.

Antisuyu was the eastern province. 'Anti' was the Quechua name for the people living here, and also means 'east.' The borders of Antisuyu reached into the edges of the Amazon jungle. 'Anti' is also the root word from which our name for the mountains, 'Andes,' takes its name. Because of contact with the Amazon, Antisuyu was the empire's doorway into the rainforests vast resources like cocoa and gold.

Kuntisuyu was the western province. 'Kunti' means west. It was the smallest of the four. It also covered a portion of Peru, including the deserts, and the area of Nazca – famous today for the Nazca lines. The steep drop to the coast meant that many important resources from the sea came from this region, and were distributed outward.

Qullasuyu was the southern and largest of the four quarters. 'Qulla' means 'south,' and stretched down the Andes into today's Chile and Bolivia. The mostly grassland region was home to the empire's agricultural center, and home to hers of llamas and alpacas.

All four of these provinces converged in Cusco, making it truly the center of the Incan world. Together, they were known as Tawantinsuyu, meaning 'The Four Regions.'

Growing Strong
Pachacuti, despite his early military success, chose instead to expand his reach by politics and peace. He had an adept network of spies, who could infiltrate the small, neighboring kingdoms and take inventory of their armies and wealth, their haves, and their needs. Pachacuti would then appeal to the leaders of these kingdoms, extolling the virtues and benefits of his empire, and how great it would profit to join him. This effective method gave Pachacuti all the advantages of expansion, without expending resources.
This also meant that the Incan Empire was a mosaic people.

Although Quechua was the official language, there were almost a dozen smaller local languages. The empire was connected by roads and trade flourished.

Foundation Myth

There is a foundation myth of the Inca Empire. Just as every civilization has a story of their first founding, the Inca story is full of magic and religion and not at all historically accurate. But understanding the Incans own beliefs as to where they originated can help understand them better as a people.

Once, before the days of the Empire, when the people of Cusco were nothing but herders and farmers, there were three caves deep in the mountains. The center cave was named Qhapaq T'uqu. The caves on its left and right were named Maras T'uqu and Sutiq T'uqu.

One day, from out of the central cave, eight humans stepped out into the sun. Four brothers, named Ayar Manco, Ayar Cachi, Ayar Awqa and Ayar Uchu. They were joined by four sisters, who went by the names Mama Ocllo, Mama Raua, Mama Huaco and Mama Qura.

The eldest brother, Ayar Manco, carried a staff made of solid gold. Imbued with magic powers, this staff would bring life wherever it struck the ground. The four brothers and four sisters traveled a long way, leaving life behind them in a trail of flourishing green.

Of the four brothers, one got on everyone's nerves more than the rest. This was Ayar Cachi, the second-eldest. He had a big mouth, constantly talking about his own great power when he was not the one who held the magic staff. Finally, the traveling companions tired of him. So they used flattery to trick him into returning to Qhapaq T'uqu, the cave from whence they came. Inside is a sacred llama, they promised, and only you have enough great power to retrieve it. A smart man would have known not to look for a llama in a cave, but Ayar Cachi fell victim to his own ego. Once inside the cave, his brothers sealed him inside and were effectively rid of him.

But in the time that had passed since the siblings left the caves, more people had begun to come from the caves on the left and right. These people are said to be the first Incas, and all further generations can trace their lineage back to these people. The youngest brother, Ayar Uchu, decided he would remain at the caves and watch over these people. So he climbed atop the cave and made a proclamation to look after and care for them. As he said it, he turned to stone, an ever-present guardian.

Ayar Auca, the third brother, decided he was tired of his family's antics. So he turned his back and went to wander alone. Ayar Manco and the four sisters were all that remained. They built a shrine around their petrified brother and then continued on their travels.

As they wandered, Ayar Manco and Mama Ocllo fell in love. They had a child together, a son named Sinchi Ruq'a. After his birth, the travelers came across the small city of Cusco. Deciding that this would be their home, Ayar Manco placed his magical golden staff into the ground.

Cusco was, at this point in time, occupied by small tribes. They did not want Ayar Manco and his companions to take their land and fought hard against the invaders. But one of the sisters, Mama Huaco, stepped up to the plate. She tied several stones together and flung them through the air, creating a staple weapon of the Incas known as bolas. The bolas hit one of the fighters, and he was instantly struck down. In fear and awe of this woman's incredible capabilities, the people of Cusco turned and ran.

From that moment on, Ayar Manco went by the name Manco Capac, and the rest is history. This legend says that he founded the Inca, rather than simply turning Cusco into a small kingdom. Whereas the real Manco Capac died peacefully in his sleep, according to legend, he turned to stone upon his deathbed like his brother.

Chapter 2: A Difficult Place to Live

Apart from the Inca Empire, no civilization has ever built itself around and atop a mountain range. Because no civilization could ever figure out how to survive on one. A mountainous race is reserved for fantasy worlds, where authors can create fictional mountain ranges filled with riches to make up for other hardships or have them populated by nonhumans entirely.

But the Incas were not Tolkien dwarves, and yet they managed to survive. Not only that, but they managed to thrive in a hostile environment. And the way they did this may seem like something out of a fantasy novel itself.

First, we need to understand the geography. At the height of its power, the Incan Empire ranged from modern Ecuador to almost the bottom of Chile. Though it did stretch itself into Bolivia and Argentina, the Incas are notable for having for length north to south than they do east to west.

The Mountains

So, why choose to stay centralized around the highest mountain range in the Western Hemisphere? After all, the Andes seem like the last choice for a settlement. Not only do they reach dangerous altitudes of 6,900 meters (over 22,000 feet) but they are part of the Pacific Ring of Fire. Volcanoes are abundant along the range.

The Andes are also famous for their varied and unpredictable weather. There are three entirely different climates found along the range: wet, dry, and tropical. In all three of these climates, air pressure and temperature drop drastically the higher you climb, and the snow line – that is, the elevation at which snowfall begins to occur – is variant depending on location.

The Wet Andes is the southernmost part of the range, reaching all the way to Cape Horn at the bottom tip of South America. They have a high rainfall and cold temperatures, meaning most of it is covered in glaciers. There is little to no plant life, making it nigh inhospitable for human settlements.

The Dry Andes takes up most of the middle of the mountains and has a semiarid desert climate. This means that it suffers through low precipitation and a lack of vegetation. The only flora to grow is stubbly, such as grass or shrubs. Like deserts, semiarid landscapes are known for hot days and cold nights. On top of this, there are several glaciers situated in the mountains, some reaching close to 10 km (6 miles) in length.

Finally, the Tropical Andes is the largest and northernmost portion. There are high peaks, valleys, and canyons, all covered in forests. The type of forest changes as the elevation gets higher. At its lowest point, the Tropical Andes is a tropical rainforest, with very high precipitation and is always hot. As the tree climb higher, they become a cloud forest. These rainforests can be easily visualized by their name alone: it is a forest, and it is cloudy. High temperatures combined with closer cloud cover means the area is densely foggy, and the natural evolution of the trees has made them gnarled and hunched over. Everything about cloud forests gives them an otherworldly, ethereal look. Finally, at its highest points, the Tropical Andes resemble something closer to the Dry Andes, with a steppe climate.

With so many rapid changes in weather and climate, most other budding civilizations would have packed up and left to find another home. So why didn't the Incas? The area provided uncomfortable living conditions and a lack of area for farming and agriculture. Were they just so stubborn that they refused to leave? The truth is, perhaps they might have tried to migrate. But any direction they could have gone in would create just as many problems.

The Deserts
Where the Andes end, up in Peru, the coastline is an arid desert. The conditions are much more extreme than those found in the Dry Andes, with temperatures of 35 Celsius (95 Fahrenheit) on a normal day. Near the southwest Andes, too, is a desert stretch, in modern-day southern Argentina. But these areas were not uninhabited, and Peru especially had several thriving cultures before the Incas were founded. The Moche, the Nazca, and the Norte Chico civilization all lived in the deserts and saw no reason to migrate away from their hot homeland.

The Jungle
Any climb down the Andes, if it didn't lead to a desert, it led to a jungle. South America is known for its tropical rainforests, most famously the Amazon that stretches across Brazil to Bolivia. Like the jungles covering the Tropical Andes, the humidity is stifling. But the tropical rainforest has the added bonus of predators. The Amazon itself is home to jaguars, anacondas, piranhas, on top of a variety of poisonous bugs and amphibians. Most tribes inhabiting the jungle remained small and contained, even to this day.

And so, with all the problems facing the early Inca, the question seems not to be 'Why?' but 'Why not?' Like the Peruvian desert peoples and the jungle tribes, the Inca had no better chance of surviving in a new climate than they did in their own. Anywhere else they could go seemed just as frustratingly complicated. And so the Inca did what mankind is best known for: they adapted.

Ecological Adaptations

One of the most primary farming adaptations made by the Andean people was to plant crops at several different elevations. By doing this, they could test the variables of weather, altitude, and soil quality. When it came to cultivating food, the main staple of the Andean diet was squash. Because the fruit has a thick skin and grows better in harsher climates, squash was popular all over the Americas. Alongside beans and maize, the Andean cultures were able to build a healthy and rich diet with little need for meat. Maize, which was developed by the Mayans in around 6,000 BCE in Mexico, was introduced to the continent of South America through trade.

Andean civilizations built their diets this way because there was a lack of large animals for food sources. South America had no horses, cattle, pigs or sheep. All the Andeans really had were llamas. Despite their usefulness as a meat source, llamas were also naturally very trainable animals and were equally useful as packers.

So due to these two factors, the early Andean people developed to be an agricultural-based society instead of hunting-based. This development would stick even as the Inca Empire rose to its greatest heights. And yet, it was not this alone that caused the Inca people to be so well-adapted to their environment. Just as the squash adapted to survive the high altitudes, so did the Inca.

Evolutionary Adaptations
All across the world, we see humans evolve to fit their surroundings. Levels of melanin in the skin change to protect a skin's exposure to the sun, becoming darkest in the areas around the equator. Humans that live in colder areas develop more body hair. It is the same way animals adapt to their surroundings, evolutionary traits changing to better survive the surrounding conditions.

But the Andean people should be noteworthy for their adaptations because they exhibited some of the most extreme examples:

One of the main problems faced by higher altitudes is the air pressure or lack of it. The higher you rise, the thinner the air, and so the less oxygen your body can take in. When your brain isn't receiving the amount of oxygen it needs, you feel faint or dizzy. Many hikers who travel the Andes report these conditions and travel guides advise you to take the ascent slowly because ascending too quickly can be damaging to your blood pressure.

As there is less oxygen, your heart rate increases in an attempt to get more blood flow to the brain. Thin, in turn, causes shallow breathing, which only further detriments the lack of oxygen. This is also why high altitudes can be dangerous to anyone with high blood pressure, pre-existing medical conditions, or pregnancy. And for healthy humans, sometimes the altitudes can be even worse, as more muscle mass means your body is struggling to spread oxygen all over this larger area.

But the Incan people had a lung capacity 1/3 the size of a regular human. This meant that on a normal breath, they could take in three times the amount of oxygen. Incans also developed to be shorter in stature, meaning there was less distance for blood to travel. Their heart rates were slowed, dealing with the body's insistence to increase heart rate at heights.

Incans also had more blood volume, almost 2 liters worth. This meant they had a higher count of red blood cells, and with that comes more hemoglobin. More hemoglobin meant more oxygen could be transferred from the blood into the tissue. Incas also had more capillaries, reaching more blood through more of their skin.

So with these kinds of evolutionary adaptations, it's no wonder the Incas managed to become the dominant civilization in South America. No other grouping of people across the world has developed quite so specifically to live in hostile environments. It was, quite literally, an uphill battle against nature, and the Inca Empire came out on top.

Chapter 3: A Day in the Life

Even though their main method of recording information is a lost system, we still know a surprising amount about Incan society. This has mostly to do with the stories passed down, and the art left behind. Some parts of the Incan taxing system were even adapted, albeit to a much crueler extent, by the Spaniards.

With the remaining information resources combined with years of study, historians and anthropologists have pieced together a very clear image of a day in the life of Inca Empire. Still, all of this knowledge must be taken with a grain of salt. For all their years of study, a historian could not travel back in time. Information ranges from having concrete evidence to being hypotheses and conjecture. Take, for example, historian's guess on the empire's population. Despite the Incans taking very careful census reports, they were recorded on quipus. The estimate ranges from 4 million to 38 million.

The most important thing to remember when studying Incan society is to remember how their economy worked. Unlike most of the rest of the world, Incans did not use a money-based payment system. Instead, they paid in labor. The population was contracted to work for the government, providing goods and services. In return, the government distributed those goods back to the population. This meant trade was well-regulated throughout the empire and it was part of government policy that no one would go unclothed, unsheltered, or unfed. This curious system has baffled outsiders since the first Spaniards made contact, and yet, it seems to have worked wonders for the rich empire.

Clothing

Like many cultures, clothing played an important part in signifying an Incan's status in society. The quality of the cloth and the amount of jewelry and regalia was determined by your standing.

Wool was the primary textile. This was practical, both for the temperature drops of the mountains and because of the abundance of wool-producing animals. For the common folk, llama wool was used. Alpaca was common for an upper-middle-class family. Reserved for the nobility were the finer wools of the vicuña and the guanaco, two native Andean camelids closely related to llamas and alpacas. And in the areas with higher temperatures, especially closer to the desert, it was more common to use cotton.

Woven into the textiles were a variety of beautiful patterns, which were not restricted to social rank. Although the most skilled weavers were always sent to Cusco to weave for the nobility, clothing was distributed by the government and so always came from a reliable source. The most common patterns were quilted squares, but it was also found that geometric patterns resembling the Nazca lines would be woven in, or designs of animals. Inca fabrics were bright and colorful, and sharing these rich fabrics with new territories was one way the Inca invited people to join their empire.

Men and women wore a very similar tunic, which consisted of a single piece of sleeveless fabric wrapped around the body and pinned together at the shoulder. The main difference lies in the length. Women's tunics reached down to their feet, while men's were shorter, and worn with breeches underneath. Both men and women wore woolen cloaks for extra warmth.

Since the weather could get so cold, the Incans could not rely merely on sandals as many previous civilizations had for centuries. Instead, Incan shoes were made of llama hide and fur. When sandals were worn, they too were made with llama hide.

Because the government controlled the distribution of clothing, a strange double-edged sword was created. While it did mean that no one ever went without clothing, it also meant that clothing had to be completely worn through or outgrown before new clothing was given.

Ornamentation wasn't reserved for the nobility, though they certainly had more of it. Because the Incans did not use a classic money system, metals and gemstones were not as highly valued as they became in other societies. But there were still differences that would mark the ranks of class. The most ornamentation to be found on commoners were the pins that held tunics and cloaks together. For women, these pins doubled in function as a knife to assist with household activities.

Noblemen wore a type of turban called a llawt'u. These headwraps came with tasseled fringe. Precious stones adorned the cloaks and tunics of the upper class, and the royalty would often line the edges of cloth with gold. Royalty and nobility wore feathered headdresses, and the feathers used were dependant on station.

The most extravagant example of clothing comes from the Sapa Inca, who never wore the same cloth twice. After wearing a tunic just once, it would be burned. Thus, weavers were needed to supply him constantly. One example of taxation of the Incan government was the service of a territory's best weaver. She would be brought to Cusco and set up to live in a temple with other chosen women. This was a highly honored position.

Food
Because of the vast difference in biomes, the empire covered, and the many highways and trade routes between major cultural centers, the diet of the Incans were colorful and diverse. Like all civilizations of the Americas, they rested on the three staples: maize, squash, and beans, a tradition carried down from their ancestors before the empire was founded.

But the agricultural exploits of the Incan Empire grew to include coca leaves, tomatoes, potatoes, avocado, and peanuts. Meat was primarily llama or alpaca, but fish could be brought up from the coat. Due to the distance, it needed to travel, fish was mostly dried. Alongside them would come dried seaweed. Chili peppers became an important part of their diet, so highly valued that entire dishes began to be designed around it.

Hunting was, as everything, controlled by the state. The meat went into the storehouses to be later distributed. As for what game could be hunted, guanaco and vicuña alongside several species of deer, and chinchillas were abundant in the mountains. On the coast, a variety of limpets, rays, and sharks were fishermen's targets, alongside seabirds, sea lions, and even dolphins. Nothing was off-limits for the Incan people, and they found nutrition wherever they could.

The skill of the Incan storehouses is still a marvel to this day. The 'qollqa,' built in mass amounts all across the empire, used the advantage of cool weather on hillsides. Using a combined method of drainage and ventilation, food in these storehouses could be kept for up to two years. Since the unstable climate could lead to flooding, drought, and other natural disasters, the careful rationing of this food meant the suppliers could continue to distribute food during times of famine.

Government

The Incans had an early federalist government. Each of the four regions was divided into constituents, called 'wapani.' Although the Sapa Inca was the divine leader, with a complete and total monarchy, he had an array of government officials to help him along.

Second to the emperor only was the high priest, who went by the title 'Willaq Umu.' As religion was so closely tied to affairs of state, the two worked together on every matter. Just below them was a kind of prime minister, an advisor known as the 'Inkap Rantin.' A kind of grand council existed under these three, with sixteen nobles from the various part of the empire: four from Cusco, four each from the larger regions of Chinchasuyu and Qullasuyu, and two each from the smaller regions of Kuntisuyu and Antisuyu.

Besides the council, each region had a kind of governor known as the Apu. The wapani of each region had their own sub-governors who reported to the Apu, called the Toqriqok. Beneath them even still, every wapani had an array of officers, record keepers, and functionaries who existed to maintain infrastructure.

Law was enforced, but the laws were simple. There were three primary principles that the Incas followed: do not steal, do not murder, and do not be lazy. The lawmen officiated capital punishment, meaning there was no prison or trial system. However, the degree to which punishment was dealt out depended on whom the crime was committed. Any crime against royalty or the noble class would be punished swiftly and immediately, while those against commoners could find leniency. In general, the decision rested with the local Toqriqok.

All in all, the government system of the empire remained largely uncomplicated, and yet despite the total control held by the Sapa Inca, it seems great care was taken to make sure the common folk had their voices heard. Simple, yet effective seems the way they went.

Architecture
The Incans have been subjected to conspiracy theorists in recent years, who believed their precision cut building blocks could only have been accomplished by the use of modern technology – or extraterrestrial help. But in actuality, the Incans were just quite ingenious when it came to their architecture.

Like the effectiveness of the storehouse, Incan buildings were made to sustain. Each stone was cut to fit exactly into the one below. This was accomplished by repeatedly pushing a block to the one below, and chiseling away at the places where they found resistance. These blocks squeezed together so well that even without the use of mortar to glue them together the walls held.

Given the situation of the Andes on a subduction zone, and the Pacific Ring of Fire to boot, earthquakes were quite common, and so all buildings needed to be structurally sound enough to resist. Amazingly, the techniques of Incan masonry provided just that. Walls had little to no points of stress concentration, meaning there was no weak spot that a shaking ground could exploit.

Stones were mostly limestone, with some granite, two sources that would have been abundant. Since the Incans had no wheel, these blocks needed to be transported by man or pack. It is believed that the hardworking and labor-centric lifestyle of the Incans is what led to their amazing teamwork and dedication. Though today we see ruins as being chalky white or grey-brown, back in their glory days they would have been painted an array of bright colors.

Medicine
The introduction of the coca leaf to the rest of the empire was perhaps life-changing if the people at the time did not know it. Grown naturally in the jungles of the Amazon, cultivation of the plant quickly spread across the mountains. Today, the coca might be best known for its use as the main ingredient of the drug cocaine. It is also easily recognized as one-half of a popular soda brand, Coca-Cola.

In its natural form, the coca leaf contains several natural alkaloids that stimulate the brain, chasing away fatigue and hunger. Believed to be divine in nature, consumption of the leaf was initially restricted to the upper class. But because of the hardworking nature of Inca society, chewing on the coca leaf while working became a central part of daily life. Yet, despite its connections to the cocaine drug, coca in its natural form has no addictive properties. Consumption of the leaf can be likened to today's use of caffeine to keep alert through work hours.

On top of acting as a stimulant, the coca leaf provided the

Inca with a variety of medicinal purposes. It was a remedy for altitude sickness, useful for travelers from the outlands climbing to cities like Cusco. It also found use as an anesthetic, for anything from headaches to childbirth. Most notably, it was used during the surgical procedure known as trepanation.

One of the longest-lasting types of pre-modern medical procedures, trepanation is the practice of drilling a small hole in the skull to relieve fluid buildup. Although it does nothing to help migraines or epilepsy, as was believed, it was effective against head wounds or fractured skulls gained from battle.

Stages of Life
For an Incan, there were seven stages of life one passed through. These stages were equal between men and woman because Incan society was fairly equality driven. Although women were relegated to housework, their role was in no way seen as inferior, and a woman was just as valuable as a man.

The first stage of life lasted three years and covered infancy. Because of the harsh conditions of the Andes, the infant mortality rate was very high, and babies were not named until their third birthday. This stage of life was called 'Wawa.'

Ages three through seven was the stage known as 'Ignorance,' or in Quechua, 'Warma.' This ignorance was seen as something every child would overcome with growth and experience. Though some translations name this stage as 'not speaking,' it is unbelievable that a child at age 7 would not be speaking fluently.

The third stage covered the next seven years, until the age of 14. It is during this time that the stages begin to have different names for boys and girls. For boys, the development stage was called 'Thaski,' and for girls, it was 'Maqt'a.' The reason for this divergence in names is due to the roles each gender played. This was around the time education would start for boys to become hunters or farmers, and women to learn the art of running a household: cooking, childrearing, and weaving.

The stage is known as 'Sipas' for men, and 'Wayna' for women was an interesting period, defining the age of sexual maturity before marriage. The Incans are noteworthy for their lax views on sex before marriage. No degree of abstinence was expected, for men or women. There was also a high degree of fairness at work when it came to marriage. The age of marriage was usually around 20 for men and 16 for women, though neither of these was rigid laws. Marriage itself was more of a contract and not based on love. However, it was not a binding contract. After the wedding came a trial period, and if one or both participants felt it wasn't going to work between them, the marriage could be annulled with no harm done to either man or woman's reputation.

The longest stage of life, and the general all-encompassing adulthood. This began at the age of around 20 when a person was married. It lasted all the way until age 70. For men, this stage was called 'Warmi.' For women, it was 'Qhari.' As with the previous stage, the age could differ between men and women, as the age of marriage skewed younger for women than it did men.

From ages 70 to 90, the stage of life when most passed away of natural causes, men were called 'Paya' and women

'Machu.' The meaning of these titles, 'Infirmity,' indicates some level of retirement among Incan families, where the younger members would care for the elderly in their household.

Finally, if a person could live this long, there is one final term for them: 'Ruku,' an unfortunate word meaning 'decrepit.' A person would stay in this stage until their death, which usually did not take long.

Life of a Noble
Despite this insistence the society had on hard work, even to the point of having a law forbidding laziness, the nobility spent an extreme amount of time being lazy. Likely, as is the case with most class systems, the top of the pyramid didn't believe the rules applied.

Instead, most of an Inca nobleman's daily life seems dedicated to one thing: making themselves better looking. Their daily lives were filled with luxury, eating the best foods, wearing the best clothes, and piercing themselves with the finest jewelry. At the very least, a man's duties would include learning the art of war, as the Sapa Inca often went on the front lines himself, and his generals were usually members of his family. Incan noblewomen, on the other hand, seem like little more than trophy wives. Their sole function was to look pretty and bear children. Still, thanks to the Incans relative belief in equality, noblewomen's duties were not viewed as lesser to her male counterpart.

The Inca is one of the cultures who practiced cranial deformation. This is the method of tying a board to a baby's head and reshaping the skull into an elongated point. Although this practice seems particularly cruel today, it was all done in the hopes of making one more attractive. An elongated skull was a sign of nobility to the Inca, the same way weight indicated good health in various European societies. When children are young, their bones are still soft and flexible, allowing this deformation to happen. As expected, this practice caused great pain to the child, and when they grow old enough, some rejected the practice entirely.

This strange shape is also found in the crystal skulls, carvings of crystal quartz that surfaced in the 1800s and were claimed to be from pre-Columbian societies. These skulls were a complete farce, of course, one of many ruses made by to sell 'real Native artifacts' to museums and archaeologists. And it is thanks to the crystal skull that the truth of the Inca Empire – and many other pre-Columbian civilizations to boot – became clouded by modern myths and pop culture, including the popular notion that the Inca were in contact with extraterrestrial life. There is no more evidence that aliens visited the Andes than there is anywhere else in the world, which is to say, very little and all speculation. Still, the belief that the crystal skulls are real and have paranormal abilities continues to this day.

Life of a Commoner

A commoner's life was much more practical. The Incan working class lived in family units, in houses situated around a farm. Men had jobs as either a farmer, a hunter, a builder, or an artisan, while women were weavers and cooks. The large family units meant that there was always more than one person to work the family farm, and households could include a variety of workers.

A type of conscription existed, taking one boy from every

family to join the army, and one girl to be a weaver in the capital. This was not to say that multiple sons from a family could join the army, as long as there were still sons to tend to the household. Again, Incan households had big families.

When a woman married, she joined the household of her husband. But there are some records of laws indicating that women inherited land from their mother. Exactly how this worked is unclear, but it could be that the land she inherited went with her into the new household. See, most commoner did not live in the city. That was reserved for the nobility, the government, and the craftsmen who directly served the upper class. Commoners instead lived outside the city, in the farmlands, and a family could work several crops unconnected to their house. Regardless, this is yet another example of the Incans having a relative measure of equality between men and women.

Other jobs to be undertaken were that of a miner. Stones always needed to be quarried for building, and learning the art of perfectly fitting the building blocks together could take years to perfect. Mining for minerals and metals was also an important undertaking. To supply the upper class with the ornamentation their station so desired, miners uncovered gold, silver, copper, tin, and gemstones such as emerald and rose quartz.

In all, Inca society was fascinatingly unique. Moreover, it is so different from what many envision thanks to the common association between the Mayans and the Aztecs. Although human sacrifice did exist within the Inca Empire, it was practiced to a much lesser extent than the Mayans, and especially the Aztecs. On the other hand, despite the Incans apparent beliefs in equality, they never let a woman take the role of Sapa Inca, unlike both Mayans and Aztecs who had several female rulers over the course of history. So, too, should the Inca Empire be remembered as something different from the surrounding cultures of the time.

If it were not for the destruction of the recording system, both of the physical quipus and the knowledge of how to decipher them, we would know much more about the ins and outs of an everyday Incan's life. Much of it is conjecture, and some conflicting reports indicate that previous guesses may have been far off from the truth. There is no knowledge of how differing sexuality was viewed, or if the gender binary was as strictly enforced as we assume it to be. We know nothing about what the life of a princess would have entailed. The ongoing study into the history of the empire is the most we will ever get, but there is the hope that the science and technology of the future could provide a more in-depth look or a differing viewpoint.

Chapter 4: The Gods

Like most old-world civilizations, the Inca were polytheistic and worshipped a variety of gods. The foremost of these was Inti, the sun god. The Sapa Inca line was said to be descended from him, a claim made popular by Pachacuti. It was in the interest of keeping this bloodline pure that, by the 15th century, it was common practice for Incan royalty to wed brother to sister.

Apart from Inti, there were a vast array of gods, all of whom would be regularly sacrificed to. Llamas were the chosen animal for sacrifice, and lore dictated that different color coats signified which llamas were sacred to which god. White llamas, for example, were reserved for sacrifice to Inti.

Inti
The aforementioned chief god, and god of the sun. Many polytheistic cultures have a sun god as their central figure, given that the sun represents life-giving and creation. This is especially true for an agriculturally-based society like the Inca since the sun is needed for all main food sources to grow. Into was represented in art as a sun with a human face, wavy lines signifying his rays.

Solar eclipses were seen as the rare manifestation of Inti's anger. The sacrifice would increase, as a way to appease him. Since solar eclipses always end, the Inca believed their methods worked. He had many temples dedicated to him, the foremost of these was the Coricancha temple complex. Located in Cusco, it was the residence of the High Priest of the Sun, the Willaq Umu.

On the longest day of winter, when the sun was least in the sky, there was a great festival held in Inti's honor. As the Incan Empire resides in the Southern Hemisphere, this was on June 21. The festival, named Inti Raymi, would last several days past the solstice. It was common to see celebrators wearing gold sun masks representing Inti, and sacrifice to him would increase.

Pachamama

She was the great earth goddess. As the one who presided over the green earth and all its bounty, she also served as a fertility goddess. Today's representation of 'Mother Earth' owes much to her, as in Quechua, Pachamama literally means 'world mother.'

As one of the primary gods of the Incan religion, Pachamama was worshipped year-round. But during August, reverence to her increased. August, as the first month of spring, was the beginning of the sowing season. Prayers were sent up that the seeds would take root and the crops would be bountiful. A special ceremony was held on July 31: families would stay up all night, cooking until dawn. As the sun first drew over the horizon, a circle was dug into the dirt. If the soil that turned up was good and healthy, it promised a good year. A plate of food is them poured into a local river, and a prayer is said. Only then may the family eat.

In her anger, Pachamama would create the earthquakes. It was believed that if too much were taken from the earth, Pachamama would be weakened and angry and thusly retaliate. Thus, it was always important to the Inca that they were giving just as much to Pachamama as they took, and that they never took more than they needed.

Mama Quilla

This goddess of the moon was Pachamama's other child and Inti's sister-wife. She was the protector of women, marriage, and presided over the menstrual cycle. She cried tears made of silver, and so silver was sacred to her, and discs of silver would be used to represent her.

Because the moon was a cycle that could follow a month, Mama Quilla was seen as a timekeeper. Thus her godly duties extended to the calendar, and she was in charge of feast days and festivals. She also had several temples dedicated to her, all tended to faithfully by her priestesses.

Unlike her husband, Mama Quilla did not succumb to anger. Lunar eclipses were instead seen as an animal attacking her. Mama Quilla was incredibly beautiful, and every so often, an animal – be it a mountain lion, fox, snake, or something else – would fall madly in love with her and jump into the sky to be with her. The Incans, to save Mama Quilla, went out into the night to make noise, to try and scare the animal away. It was thought that, if the animal could not be frightened and the moon's light never returned, the world would be dark forever.

Illapa

Alongside Inti and Mama Quilla, this god was one of the three central gods of Incan religion. He reigned over the sky, the clouds, thunder and lightning, and rain. He was represented in art as a man, walking about the sky in a shining cloak, with a war club and sling in hand.

As the weather across the empire was so wild and important to agricultural output, Illapa was extremely important. He controlled the rain, and so could control when a drought would blight the land. He could also call up the great thunderstorm. Lightning was his shining cloak, and the sound of thunder came from the crack of his sling.

He had a temple in Coricancha, tended to by his priests. His effigy within the temple had a headdress draped over his face, to represent clouds, veiling the storm and his anger.

Supay

Every polytheistic religion had a god of death, but the lengths to which they revered or feared this death dog varied widely. For the Inca, their death god came in the form of Supay, it was a fair and healthy mix of both.

The Inca world was divided into three spheres: the skies above where most of the gods resided, the earth where humans lived, and the land underground. This last realm, called Uku Pacha, was a place where the dead and demons resided. Supay was a hideous, gnarled, deformed figure, and he was said to come up to the mortal world in the form of a snake to watch over babies, wishing they would join him.
But how much of this bad reputation is true to Incan beliefs and how much was due to Catholic twisting is unclear. Whenever European settlers came into contact with a new polytheistic religion, they tried to equate it to their own beliefs. Thus Supay, like many other death gods before him, was equated with the Devil. This influence can be seen even today, where masks of him are portrayed with great devil horns.

The Andean people had an infamously high infant mortality rate, to the point that they did not even name children until their second birthday, so it is no wonder the story about Supay watching over children came to be. Believing that the god of death was fond of children and only wanted to take care of them was surely a way to help ease the pain of the death of a child.

Ekeko

When in need of good fortune, prayers would be sent to Ekeko. He was the god of prosperity, and predated the Inca Empire, receding all the way back to the Tiwanaku Empire. Always portrayed as smiling and with a smoke between his lips, Ekeko was truly a jolly god.

He is mostly presented in the form of an amulet, like a good luck token. Today, you are still likely to find a little statue of him kept in houses, as a way to bring good fortune to your family.

Chasca

Goddess of the dawn and twilight, patron of the morning and evening star, Chasca was also a goddess of beauty. She served as a protector of young girls before marriage.

The planet Venus, also known as the morning star and the evening star, is one of the planets visible to the naked eye. In almost every culture around the world, this star is associated with a goddess of the dawn, which usually symbolizes love and fertility on top. The Incans were no different. Chasca Was also associated with spring and renewal, so offerings to her would be filled with flowers.

Catequil

A complicated guy, Catequil was the god of thunder and lighting. Due to the much more prominent Illapa already being the god of storms, it was likely Catequil began as a local god from another tribe that joined the Inca Empire.

Incan mythology has little to no evidence of demigods, or children born from the union of a god and a mortal. The closest to this was the belief that the Sapa Inca was descended from Inti, but this was not believed to be due to a union with a mortal woman. Inti and Mama Quilla were the parents of Manco Capac, according to legend, and his mortality is unclear.

But there is some evidence to suggest that, where he was worshipped, Catequil was the father of all twins. The belief held that Catequil came to earth in the form of a lightning bolt and had relations with a mortal woman, and this resulted in twins. It is not known whether this belief was upheld all over the empire, or only in certain places. It makes one wonder what the rationale behind triplets was.

Pacha Kamaq

He began as a local god worshipped in the city-state of Pachacamac, by the Ichma people. Pacha Kamaq was their creator deity, and the city was named for him.

Like many small tribal gods, Pacha Kamaq was absorbed into the Incan pantheon when the state was merged with the empire. But what makes him noteworthy among the others is that Pacha Kamaq was raised to quite high importance. He was married to Pachamama. Sometimes he was portrayed as Inti's father, likely a confusion with another creator deity, Viracocha. Other portrayals have him as Inti's son. This confused placement within the pantheon signifies his origin in another place. It also highlights his popularity, and how the mythos attempted to insert him into such important positions.

Viracocha

The god of the skies and all creation. Initially, Viracocha was the primary deity worshipped by the Inca. But when Pachacuti was crowned Sapa Inca, he promoted Inti to the position, and Viracocha gradually moved away from the focus.

But that is not to say that he didn't retain his importance. The story given was that he taught the first Andean people everything they needed to know, then retreated across the Pacific to spread knowledge to other cultures. As is the case with many disappearing religious figures, Viracocha promised to one day return.

Viracocha is widely regarded to have been the father of Inti and Mama Quilla, but there are some disputes. He remains mysterious, a name that was clearly important enough for the eights Sapa Inca – and Pachacuti's father himself – to have been named after him. Renderings of him in art strive to show his all-encompassing range and his importance over every other god, from wearing the sun as a crown, to the very rain being his tears. In each of his hands, he held a thunderbolt.

Mama Qucha

The goddess of the sea, patron to the fisherman. All creatures that lived beneath the waves were in her domain. She was the wife of Viracocha, and the mother of Inti and Mama Quilla.

But she was not only worshipped in the coastal regions. Mama Qucha was not the goddess of merely the sea, but of all bodies of water, fresh or salt. So lakes, rivers, and even man-made drainage channels were all under her domain.

What is truly amazing about Mama Qucha is that her sphere of influence tells us that the Incans understood the water cycle. They knew that runoff would return to the sea and that the same water would return to the clouds, and fall again as precipitation. For a society that had no scientific explorations and had not even use of the wheel, it is fascinating that a religious figure would help pass on such knowledge.

Alongside these, there were a variety of minor gods. Most of these minor deities, like Pacha Kamaq, were assimilated into the empire alongside their people. But worship for them remained fairly local. The Inca Empire was similar enough to the Roman Empire in this regard, never forcing a community to give up their own gods, only asking that the Incan gods also be worshipped, and held in highest regard.

Sacrifice

It's impossible to talk about any pre-Columbian religion without talking about one of their most sacred tenants: sacrifice. This was an unfortunate practice that no native Mesoamerican or South American civilization seems to have missed.

Though human sacrifice is found all over the world, it seems to be mostly associated today with the Mayans, the Aztecs, and the Inca. This is thanks to the Aztecs and their most extreme example of pulling out a human heart, a vivid image that doesn't leave the mind once it has entered. The Inca did not practice this, in particular, but rather had their own way of sacrificing.

Usually, when sacrifice is mentioned in this book, it means the sacrifice of food, drink, or personal items. These were the most common forms of sacrifice, and the ones practiced at every ritual. Animals were also common, mostly the abundant llama. But the Incans did engage in something they called 'Qhapaq Hucha,' and it was a form of child sacrifice.

The practice was rationalized as the Incans sending their best children to join the gods. The chosen were drugged with a combination of coca leaves and chicha, an alcoholic beverage. These children, who were well-fed before the sacrificial walk beforehand to ensure their happiness, were sent to the highest point on the mountains they could reach. They were sent with the finest clothing, jewels and other artifacts, and more delicious food. They would die on the mountains.

The weather conditions of the Andes have led to the discovery of mummified children in the mountainous peaks. These include Momia Juanita, whose body is on display at the Museo Santuarios Andinos in Peru. But most famous of these is the perfectly preserved 14-year-old girl known only as The Maiden. Her body sits at the High Mountain Archaeological Museum in Argentina. Despite the sadness that comes with finding such bodies, their mummified state allowed anthropologists and historians to learn new things about Incan society.

Unlike the future Spaniards, the Incan war was never really driven by religious movement. When the empire did go to war, it was usually because their treaty negotiations didn't work.

War Boys
One of the notable points of interest about Incan battle tactics was their tendency to peacock. Even after marching an army all the way to a destination, Incans would try to impress their enemies into submission with displays of

strength. In a way, this is just another part of their negotiations. Pachacuti's style of enticing others to join the empire relied on assuring the outside force that their state would only benefit from making the decision. By displaying such military power, the Incans were assuring their enemies that this was the power they could be a part of. They did not have to fight, but could instead choose to be on the winning side. It is not known how often this succeeded, but it clearly did not work every time.

When they were called to battle, the Incan armies employed tactics, not unlike those found in other early armies. The militia was divided into subsections based on weapons used. First, the projectile division would rain down spears and stones on the enemy, softening their ranks. After this, the first line would march, consisting of men with battering weapons. Most commonly used were war clubs, or a kind of mace called a macana.

While the front lines engaged the opposing army in hand to hand combat, back divisions would split apart and circle around the opposing army. These separate division would then hit the flanks, pushing the enemy in on all sides and effectively encircling them. Surrender came from the enemy generals soon after.

The Inca also had a habit of employing psychological warfare in their battles. After a show of peacocking, they would advance to the front lines of the battlefield in complete, eerie silence. Once the armies were in place, the Inca would erupt in a mass of jeering and catcalls. This could quite often unsteady their opponents, causing them to lose faith in themselves, or subconsciously believe that the Inca were unbeatable and the war was effectively already lost.

The Incans did not have a prominent god of war, showing how they were not a military-based civilization. Still, despite this, they were largely undefeated in battle. Tactics combined with the sheer mass of soldiers meant they would be at an advantage against any foe. That is, any foe native to their land.

Chapter 5: Decline and Downfall

So how did an empire so vast and so strong crumble to pieces within such a short period of time? It is often touted that Rome did not fall in a day, but the Inca Empire certainly seems to have. Surely, the invading force of a foreign nation and one with lesser numbers on top of that could not be solely responsible for such a devastation. And, partially, this is true. The Inca Empire was already beginning to fracture by the time the Spanish made contact. And there were more factors at play when it came to the invading army, more than just size. Advanced technology, weaponry, mass plague, and even understanding of the stars all contributed to the near-instant takeover of the glorious empire.

Civil War
Anytime a dynasty is based on a royal bloodline, a war for succession is guaranteed to break out. The Inca Empire was no different. The line of Pachacuti began to crumble in 1527, upon the death of his grandson, Huayna Capac.

Like most Sapa Inca before him, Huayna Capac was married to his full-blooded sister, Coya Cusirimay. As is often the case with incestuous unions, the couple had trouble conceiving, and this left him with no sons born by his royal wife. They did have daughters, but none of them could be considered heirs. The title of Sapa Inca had never been, and would never be, bestowed to a woman.

Huayna Capac, however, was known for his multiple affairs and produced some 50 illegitimate sons with a variety of other women. Still, none of these sons could inherit.

Eventually, Coya Cusirimay was set aside. Huayna Capac took his younger sister, Rahua Ocllo. Finally, he had a trueborn son and heir, Ninan Cuyochi.

But death lingered on the horizon for this family. In 1526, the Spanish conquerors were making their way south in search of greater riches. Huayna Capac traveled to meet them, and though this delegation was peaceful in nature, the great Sapa Inca contracted smallpox. That small moment of interaction was all it took to send a dynasty crumbling. Huayna Capac died shortly after, alongside his brother – and his heir, Ninan Cuyochi.

With his sudden death, Huayna Capac had left no instructions for the line of succession. The Incans were unprepared for a situation like this, and it was unclear to whom the title should pass. Two choices were put forward. The first was Huascar, the younger brother of Ninan Cuyochi, born to the royal wife, Rahua Ocllo. The second option was Atahualpa, one of Huayna's illegitimate sons.

The nobility backed Huascar, the only option in their eyes. He was pure of blood, the rightful heir. Atahualpa, however, would have been the political choice. For during Huayna Capac's reign, he had continued the legacy of his father and grandfather by expanding and conquering new territory. The most prominent of these acquisitions was the northern province of Quito. Atahualpa's mother was a member of the demoted royal family. Thus, Atahualpa was beloved among the northern regions as a man of their people. He had also, in the years leading up to his father's death, gained popularity among the rest of the empire for being personable, intelligent, and dignified.

In an attempt to appease the common people, Atahualpa was sent to his homeland in the north to be a kind of governor. Huascar was crowned Sapa Inca. But this tentative peace could not last long. Huascar, unsecured in his place on the throne, began to fear that his half-brother would rise up against him. He demanded all his subjects pay tribute. Now, Atahualpa was more than happy and sent the newly crowned Sapa Inca tributes and messengers to extoll his loyalty. But Huascar, who was growing increasingly paranoid, saw this all as a trick. He murdered the messengers and sent them back, becoming a self-fulfilling prophecy as Atahualpa then declared war.

The following five years saw the empire ravaged with battle. Atahualpa and his forces descended south, encountering victory in almost every battle. Near 1533, Atahualpa's generals reached Cusco and seized the city. Huascar and his family were seized and killed.

This might have seen the end of the war, and the empire might have gradually returned to peace and stabilization after this. But within that five-year span, the Spanish explorers had returned to the Spanish-conquered cities in Central America, with reports of the vast wealth the city of Cusco. The Spanish army obtained a seal from the emperor, Charles I, ordering them to conquer the Incans in the name of the Spanish Empire. So the armies returned, under the leadership of conquistador Francisco Pizarro.

New Castile
Francisco Pizarro had been living in the impoverished Panama region, and it was the promise of these richer lands down south that first spurred him onward. Though the previous quest into the Andes never reached the city of

Cusco, the rumors he heard were enough for him to petition a return with reinforcements.

Upon Pizarro's return, he came across Atahualpa. Pizarro's men and their customs scared Atahualpa, and he did not know whether to drive them away or welcome them. He wasn't given much time to deliberate, because the Spanish captured him shortly afterward. While Atahualpa's men killed Huascar elsewhere, Atahualpa himself was executed.

An example of Pizarro's cunning and cruelty can be seen during Atahualpa's imprisonment. Atahualpa promised Pizarro a room full of gold for ransom if he would release him. Pizarro agreed, and the gold was delivered. Pizarro had no intention of ever releasing Atahualpa but continued to promise, allowing the gold and silver to pile up. In his greed, he wanted to keep Atahualpa alive so the riches would keep coming. But his men demanded the execution, and so eventually Pizarro complied.

The Incan Empire had already suffered one succession crisis that led to the civil war and now faced another. As the Spanish took advantage of the weakened defenses, they entered Cusco and placed Yupanqui, the younger brother of Atahualpa, on the throne.

Much of the nobility saw the Spanish as liberators, here to put an end to the civil war and restore peace to their empire. They welcomed the Spanish and celebrated their new Sapa Inca. But what the nobles did not realize at first was that Yupanqui was nothing but a puppet, a face Pizarro could put on the throne to earn the loyalty of the native people. In practice, the Inca Empire was now under the complete control of Pizarro. In the grand tradition of renaming native regions 'New' Christian city, the area was dubbed New Castile. As governor, Pizarro was tasked to give the state a new capital, to which he chose a coastal city and renamed in Lima. Now, hundreds of Spanish would pour in, taking the land for themselves and settling amongst the natives.

A Rebel with a Cause
In 1535, Pizarro left Cusco to chase one of the last remaining forces of resistance. His brothers, Juan and Gonzalo, were left behind alongside Yupanqui to maintain control. This would prove to be a mistake, as the two brothers mistreated Yupanqui. The Sapa Inca came to realize the lack of power he held in his position, and that the once-revered title had become an in-name-only clause. With only two guards on him, Yupanqui escaped into the surrounding highlands.

Now seeing the Spanish for what they truly were, Yupanqui rallied the people behind him. Spending ten months on the run, as a kind of mythical exiled prince, Yupanqui took smaller cities and eliminated small Spanish outposts. He returned to Cusco a year later with a new army behind him. At the same time, his close general and possible brother, Quiso, led a siege on the city of Lima. Both were successful. Yupanqui even managed to repel four entire reinforcement squads, until Pizarro himself was forced to return to deal with Yupanqui himself.

Pizarro's forces retook Cusco with some ease, and Yupanqui retreated to Vilcabamba, a small post in the eastern jungles of Antisuyu. He took everyone he could, from his royal family to commoners, and settled within the trees. Those around him at the time said Yupanqui considered this his final defeat, and did the best he could to turn this little settlement into the new seat for the Inca Empire. Never again would he attempt to retake his old lands.

Vilcabamba became known as the New-Inca, or New Inca kingdom, but it only lasted 33 years before it, too, was overtaken by the Spaniards. With that, the last remaining independence of the Inca Empire was snuffed out.

Steel vs. Bronze

The level of technological differences between the two forces cannot be stressed enough. During the 16th century, the Incans were still using bronze and stone weapons. They had never needed a reason to advance their weaponry. Much of Incan expansion was done through the use of political maneuvering, and when war between tribes did occur, the opposing forces used bronze and stone as well.

But by this point in time, Europe had been through countless crusades. The process of alloying iron and carbon to create steel had been perfected by everyone from the Vikings to the Indians, and it was the common metal found in weapons. The use of gunpowder from China had spread to every corner of the Eastern Hemisphere. Spain itself had lived through the Reconquista, a campaign that lasted almost 800 years.

Bronze is an alloy of copper and tin. Both of these are members of the seven metals of antiquity, metals mostly used by the ancient world. As others, both copper and tin are fairly soft and malleable. When forged together to create bronze, they are stronger than iron. Bronze was a reliable metal and had its many uses outside weaponry. But to put it in perspective, the Bronze Age ended in the year 300 – B.C.E.

Steel, on the other hand, alloys iron with carbon. Iron is a far more abundant metal than tin, and carbon could be found in a variety of places. Steel has a higher durability and is less likely to shatter upon impact. It retains an edge for longer, meaning less time is needed to maintain the upkeep of a blade. Spanish rapiers, in particular, were known for their incredible bend.

When Francisco Pizarro and his men arrived on the Andes frontier, he had one cannon, 27 horses, and 168 men at his back. Each of these men had a steel sword, steel armor, and a gun. No matter how many Incan soldiers swarmed the men, they were hopelessly outmatched. Their bolas, the stone-throwing weapons that had served head injuries for centuries, could hardly make a dent in the helmets of their adversaries.

It is also important to note that, as is so often forgotten, horses are not native to the Americas. The Incans would never have seen something like them before. The llamas and other camelids of their homelands were not large or strong enough to support a rider, so the Incan infantry had never included mounted soldiers. There were no known strategies for defending against such a force.

Bending the Gods

The Reconquista and the subsequent conquering of the New World were backed by an unwavering religious belief. The Spanish were strong in their beliefs that Christianity should be the only religion. Before it was an empire, Spain had been under the control of the Islamic Empire, and the Reconquista was the long-fought process to expel all Muslim influence and insert absolute Christian authority.

As the Spaniards assumed control of the Inca Empire, they

too the native pantheon and merged it with their own beliefs. Hence Supay became the Devil, Pachamama was the Virgin Mary, and Viracocha was the closest they had to God. This practice was common for all invading Christians, and almost every pagan religion has these influences that are still seen today.

One of the ways the Spaniards dazzled the Incans was with their knowledge of astronomy. Because they could predict when lunar eclipses would happen, priests considered them in the highest regard. It is a bit of a misconception that the Spanish annihilated the natives in a bloodbath. Their takeover was much more insidious. The newcomers were welcomed, even celebrated. Between their puppet rulers, baptisms, and intermarriages, the Spanish Empire had successfully absorbed the Inca Empire.

The Plagues
Alongside smallpox, the Spanish brought a whole host of disease that the native people's immune systems had no resistance to and no way of fighting. Typhus, measles, and the flu were three of the other most common offenders. Though most of these diseases are treatable, to the unprepared body, they were instantly fatal.

Human immune systems build resistance to bacterial infections over time. Today, immunization is achieved by inserting dead bacterial cells into the bloodstream, so white blood cells learn to recognize the disease and fight it. The native people of the Americas had no time to build an immune system. Although these diseases were just as dangerous to the Spanish and the conquistadors suffered an immense number of fatalities, it was nothing compared to the effect it had on the native population.

The diseases were not just carried to the Incans by the newcomers. Plagues had already devastated 90% of the Mesoamerican population and were now spreading south independent of the relatively small Spanish army.

If the succession crisis hadn't happened, and the Inca Empire was united under Atahualpa, perhaps the invasion would have played out differently. But while the ravaging of the civil war certainly made things easier, in the end, it's likely it wouldn't have mattered. Between war, plague, and advanced technology, the Andean people were almost completely wiped out. Along with their knowledge of the quipu went agricultural knowledge and local religions. In just a few short years, the Inca Empire had gone from one of the richest and far-reaching empires of the Western Hemisphere to near extinction.

Chapter 6: Remains of the Day

With so much creativity, color, and ingenious architecture lost to the ages, it would be easy to think that the only thing that remains of the great Inca Empire is the ruins of the city of Machu Picchu. But besides that marvel, there are so many little things the Incans left behind. Things that influence us even today, things that you might not even think to attribute to them.

Machu Picchu

Lost to the heights of the Andes after the conquest, the city of Machu Picchu was only rediscovered in 1911. Thanks to much of the destruction of classical architecture by the Spanish, it was Machu Picchu that showed the world just how precise the Inca were with their building techniques. Machu Picchu shocked the world with its beauty, splendor, and structural integrity.

Though the origins of Machu Picchu are unknown, it is widely regarded to have been commissioned by Pachacuti as a summer retreat, as a kind of vacation palace, for the royal family. It has remains of living quarters along with a temple for the god Inti and terraced fields for agriculture.

At an altitude of 2,400 meters above sea level, the existence of Machu Picchu as a vacation palace truly puts into perspective how incredible the evolutionary adaptations of the Andean people truly were. The hike to Machu Picchu today is dangerous, and many suffer from altitude sickness while trying to visit. Some with blood pressure conditions may never even get a chance to see the city, as their doctors would strongly advise against it.

But despite the conditions, for its beauty and its look into Incan architecture, Machu Picchu is the center of Peruvian tourism. The city has boosted the economy, providing the country one of its largest sources of revenue. It is also a named World Heritage Site and was recently chosen as one of the New Seven Wonders of the World.

Machu Picchu is the grandest, but not the only surviving bit of monumental Incan architecture. The Coricancha Temple in Cusco remains are fairly well-preserved, and another key part of Peru's tourism industry. Those on their way to Machu Picchu usually begin in Cusco, following the same ascent as Pachacuti and his family would have done.

Food
Many of your favourite foods to this day are likely Incan in origin. Chili peppers originate from all over the Americas, but the Inca was one of the reasons their cultivation became so common. Columbus, for all his many flaws, did manage to introduce the chili pepper to Europe.

Chicha is an alcoholic beverage fermented mostly from maize. It was the staple alcohol of the Inca, and the drink usually poured in sacrifice to the gods. It is still a popular drink to this day, and its origins have not been forgotten.

The reason we associate pumpkins and other squash with Thanksgiving is actually thanks to the Inca and other Mesoamerican civilizations. Because the squash was such an integral part of their diet, and so foreign to Columbus and his men, the imaginary image of the Thanksgiving meal between pilgrims and natives included these foods as a key component. The next time you take a slice of pumpkin pie, give thanks to the Inca.

We talked about the coca leaf and its negative effects in creating the drug cocaine. But when the soda brand Coca-Cola was founded in 1886, the two things they used to create their signature flavor was kola nuts and coca leaves. Though cola leaves are not part of the secret recipe anymore, without the Inca chewing these leaves, we wouldn't have Coke as we know it today. Perhaps because of its origin, Coke is especially popular in Central and South America today.

Language
The Quechua language is still spoken by natives in the Andean regions today, meaning that although the quipus are a lost art, not all methods of communication are gone.

It is a miracle that the language survived for all the years it did. During the 18th century and the height of Spanish occupancy, Quechua was suppressed and speaking it became outlawed. But it was the Spanish themselves who allowed the Quechuan languages to continue. Back in their earlier days of supremacy, missionaries encouraged the learning of Quechua, to better communicate with the native people. In fact, it was a Spaniard himself, Domingo de Santo Tomas, who first began to record Quechua in the Latin alphabet. He is most likely the reason we can read it today.

Thanks to the division of the Inca Empire, the Quechua languages split into two branches, known simply as Quechua I and Quechua II. The differences between these come down to the local dialect. Quechua I, also known as Central Quechuan, has speakers mostly grouped around the center of the Andes, as the name would suggest. It remains fairly uniform as all the speakers a geographically close together. Quechua II, also known as Peripheral Quechuan, is the dialect spoken in the farther reaches. Because it is so widely distributed, there are several subdivisions within the language. Some of these differences can get quite drastic. And yet, Quechuan speakers of all dialects can understand one another through the differences.

Quechua has managed to survive and to this day is spoken by more than 8 million people. It is the largest surviving language of the native Americas and is an official language of Peru and Bolivia. You can even hear it in blockbuster movies. *Star Wars* and its famous character, Greedo, used Quechuan as the basis for his alien language. The fourth *Indiana Jones* movie, which partly takes place in South America, has the famed hero speaking Quechuan with native Peruvians. And in a notable example, the Quechuan name Tupac has risen to fame today thanks to famed rapper and entertainer, Tupac Shakur.

Inti Raymi
One of the great Incan gods has not been forgotten. Inti, their most important god of the sun, has experienced a revival, especially in regards to his yearly festival. Inti Raymi has become a national holiday of Peru. Just like in the days of the Empire, the nine-day celebration begins on June 24.

If you want to witness this event today, all you need to do is visit Peru during your summer vacation. The parades in the city of Cusco are so vibrant that half the city is shut down. What is truly special about today's Inti Raymi, as well, is the regard to which it holds the native people. Dancers, singers, and entertainers from the four Incan regions are part of the procession. Every year, two Quechuan actors are chosen to portray the Sapa Inca, Manco Capac, and his consort, Mama Ocllo.

Entertainers and overseers alike dress in traditional clothing. The procession hen follows the same path it did 600 years ago when Pachacuti was the Sapa Inca. Beginning at the heart of Cusco at the Coricancha Temple, it follows all the way to the ruins of Sacsayhuaman on the outskirts of the city. Libations are poured out as a sacrifice, to honor the great god Inti. In our modern day, the celebrator is likely honoring the great people who came before them.

The actor portraying the Sapa Inca, at exactly 1:30 PM, gives a speech to the surrounding crown, and another to the watching Inti. Beer is passed around, performances are held, and the festival once again kicks into party mode.

The Goddess Cult of Pachamama
From the 1960s onward, the rising movements of Neopaganism and feminism coalesced to create a kind of modern cult that was strictly goddess-based. This modern religion has no rulebook, guidelines, or even a name, but it is used by many women who dabble in spiritualism, occultism, and naturalism. Though often parodied, such as in the 1994 hit sitcom *Friends* with its book 'Be Your Own Wind-Keeper,' the actual goddess cults of modern day are quite down to earth.

Rooted in the feminist movement and the art of building self-esteem, goddess cultism is like astrology. Believers can range anywhere from passing fancies to devoted students. Most members are just women who enjoy researching the women of the pagan pantheons. Usually stemming from a childhood fascination with a figurehead like Artemis or Freya, research into a variety of pre-Christian mythical women leads many women to direct their prayers to a patron goddess or two.

But for the New Age movement of South America, interest in the earth goddess Pachamama has increased more than almost any other. Her conflagration with the Virgin Mary means that many mestizo Andeans – that is, Andeans with mixed white and native heritage – are simultaneously Christians and pagan goddess worshippers. Interest in Pachamama has peaked across the world, and tourist guides often enthuse visitors to sacrifice drink or small items to Pachamama while in sacred sites, such as Machu Picchu. The practice is very similar to the tourism of Hawaii, which uses sacrifice to the volcano goddess Pele as a part of visiting the Kilauea crater.

Like Inti, Pachamama has her own festival today in Peru and Ecuador, known as Pachamama Raymi. Held on August 1, the festival is not quite so large as Inti Raymi, but that fact that worship of her survives is nevertheless a sign that not all of the Inca Empire is lost to the ages.

Conclusion

The tragic loss of the Inca Empire on the rest of the world cannot be overstated enough. So much culture and knowledge was lost and was doomed to be since the day Christopher Columbus set out to sea. And yet, in the face of so much adversity, some has remained to this day.

The grand history of the Andean people, from their humble beginnings to the height and glory of an ever-reaching empire, is almost too fantastic to be real. Through innovation and determination, the Andeans overcame great odds to call those Andes home. Evolutionary adaptations the likes of which can't be found in any other civilization mark the Inca as unique.

Their pantheon is fascinating and deserves the same level of study given to the Greek Olympians or the comic book featuring Norse gods. Their policy of acquiring new territory through negotiations and mutually beneficial deals, and the respect to which they showed such territories, are the kind of politics we should be adapting to fit our modern values. They should never be confused for the Mayans or the Aztecs, nor should they be touted as copycats or an offshoot that came afterward. The Inca were proud, independent, hardworking, loyal, and strong. Honor their memory by understanding them, learning their history, and sharing the knowledge with everyone you can. Visit Peru, take part in Inti Raymi and Pachamama Raymi.

And the next time you have a Coca-Cola, pour one out for the glory of the Inca Empire.

THE BYZANTINE EMPIRE

A Complete Overview Of The Byzantine Empire History from Start to Finish

© Copyright 2018 by Eric Brown

All rights reserved.

The following eBook is reproduced below with the goal of providing information that is as accurate and reliable as possible. Regardless, purchasing this eBook can be seen as consent to the fact that both the publisher and the author of this book are in no way experts on the topics discussed within and that any recommendations or suggestions that are made herein are for entertainment purposes only. Professionals should be consulted as needed prior to undertaking any of the action endorsed herein.

This declaration is deemed fair and valid by both the American Bar Association and the Committee of Publishers Association and is legally binding throughout the United States.

Furthermore, the transmission, duplication or reproduction of any of the following work including specific information will be considered an illegal act irrespective of if it is done electronically or in print. This extends to creating a secondary or tertiary copy of the work or a recorded copy and is only allowed with an expressed written consent from the Publisher. All additional rights reserved.

The information in the following pages is broadly considered to be truthful and accurate account of facts, and as such any inattention, use or misuse of the information in question by the reader will render any resulting actions solely under their purview. There are no scenarios in which the publisher or the original author of this work can be in any fashion deemed liable for any hardship or damages that may befall them after undertaking information described herein.

Additionally, the information in the following pages is intended only for informational purposes and should thus be thought of as universal. As befitting its nature, it is presented without assurance regarding its prolonged validity or interim quality. Trademarks that are mentioned are done without written consent and can in no way be considered an endorsement from the trademark holder.

Table of Contents

Introduction 67

Chapter 1: Creation, Division, and Standing Alone 68

Chapter 2: The Justinian Dynasty 75

Chapter 3: The Decline of the Empire and the Rise of Islam 82

Chapter 4: Resurgence Under the Macedonian Dynasty 89

Chapter 5: The Crusades and Their Impact 96

Chapter 6: The Fourth Crusade 103

Chapter 7: The Decline of the Empire and the Fall of Constantinople 110

Conclusion 117

Introduction

Congratulations on downloading *The Byzantine Empire*, and thank you for doing so.

The following chapters will discuss the rise and fall of one of the longest-lived empires in the history of the world. Though not as well-known today as the empire that spawned it, the Byzantine Empire stood for a thousand years as a continuation of the Roman Empire itself. From the founding of Constantinople by Emperor Constantine to the empire rising to its peaks under Justinian I and Basil II, down to its slow and tragic collapse following the sacking of Constantinople in 1204 CE, the entire history of the empire will be covered in this book.

The Byzantine Empire, having spent most of its history straddling Europe and Asia, had a tremendous impact on the culture of civilizations on both continents. As such, it should be as widely known as the other great empires in history. In part, this book intends to push a greater understanding of the second longest-lived empire in human history to a wider audience. From its cultural impact on the Ummayad Caliphate to its role in the Crusades, and to the impact of its collapse on Europe, the Byzantine Empire left its mark on multiple countries.

There are plenty of books on this subject on the market, so thanks again for choosing this one! Every effort was made to ensure it is full of as much useful information as possible. Please enjoy!

Chapter 1:
Creation, Division, and Standing Alone

It would be nearly impossible to discuss the history of the Byzantine Empire without first discussing the empire it succeeded: the Roman Empire. Founded in the final century before the Common Era, the Roman Empire was, at its peak, the most powerful political entity of its time. It controlled every territory in and around the Mediterranean Sea and spanned from Egypt to modern England. But the administrative system which had served it well during its initial two centuries eventually began to show some critical flaws.

It was under the reign of Emperor Diocletian that the idea of dividing the responsibilities of ruling the empire was first introduced. Diocletian came to power following a period of great strife for the empire known as the Crisis of the Third Century. It was a 50-year period following the death of Emperor Severus Alexander in 235 CE, which was marked by external invasions, civil wars, and economic stagnation. It briefly resulted in two large territories, the Gallic Empire and the Palmyrene Empire, breaking off from the empire. Though the empire was reunited under Emperor Aurelian, who reigned from 270-275 CE, it was not until the ascent of Diocletian in 284 CE that the empire truly recovered from the ordeal.

Due to coming to power following such a long period of crisis, Diocletian came to believe that the Roman Empire had simply outgrown the decentralized system of governance created by the first Emperor, Augustus. He sought to place more power in the hands of the Emperors to grant them the ability to rule more effectively. To this end, he instituted political reforms which ultimately marked the transition from the Principate period, wherein the Emperor was, in theory, considered first among equals amongst the senators, to the Dominate period, wherein the Emperors gradually took more and more power for themselves, often at the expense of the Senate.

The primary importance of this period to the later Byzantine Empire lay in the most vital reform made by Diocletian: the division of the empire into two distinct administrative zones. Initially naming Maximian as Caesar—or junior Emperor to his own Augustus or senior Emperor—in 285 CE, he went on to promote Maximian to Augustus the next year and declared that both men would choose their own Caesars to aid in the administration of the empire more directly. He took over the control of the Eastern Roman Empire, leaving the western half to Maximian. Though the Tetrarchy, or the "rule of four" as it was also known, did not last long following the retirement of its first two Augusti, it was important for having formalized the division between the culturally similar yet distinct eastern and western halves of the empire.

The simple fact that the pair retired was significant in itself, and the rarity of such an event likely contributed to the reasons why the system that Diocletian created failed to outlast him. It was a very old Roman concept—a public servant dedicating their time to truly serve the public and then retiring when they feel they could no longer work as well as they used to. It was actually seldom followed, and even the Roman Emperors who weren't killed either in battle against the empire's enemies or during civil conflicts more often than not died in office. The Tetrarchy did not live long past the reign of Diocletian because it had been him, in large part, who made the system effective: he was unusually dedicated to serving the public good over his own interests. Diocletian, in 305 CE, became the first Emperor to abdicate willingly. He then spent the final six years of his life retired in peace, tending a vegetable garden.

The reign of Constantine was by far the most important early influence on the later Byzantine Empire. Coming to power as Caesar in the west in 306 CE, he became the unquestioned Augustus by 312 CE. He ruled peacefully alongside the Augustus in the east Licinius for two years, but starting from 314 CE, the two became increasingly hostile rivals for power. In 321 CE, outright civil war broke out between them, and it ended in 324 CE following Constantine's victory at the Battle of Chrysopolis.

The civil war between the two emperors was seen at the time as a religious conflict between the Christian and Latin west and the pagan and Greek east. It was determined that to facilitate the reintegration of the Greek east into the empire, a new eastern capital needed to be established. To this end, Constantine chose the site of Byzantium and raised it as his own new capital. In 330 CE, Constantinople was established, marking the beginning of a permanent divide between the east and west that would be formalized some sixty-five years later.

Two other vital changes made by Constantine played a part in the history of the later-divided empire: the establishment of a hereditary succession tradition and the legalization of Christianity. Once it's been legalized, Christianity's leaders quickly moved to replace paganism as the dominant religion within the empire. Their success had been so rapid that by 395 CE, Emperor Theodosius I was able to outlaw paganism outright. Theodosius I was also able to leave the succession to his two sons without a significant civil conflict breaking out as a consequence—a testament to the success of the other major change made by Constantine.

Theodosius' sons, Arcadius and Honorius, inherited the Eastern and Western Roman Empires, respectively, and it was their reigns which marked the permanent division of the two halves. Arcadius and his successors would rule over the Eastern Roman Empire well beyond the fall of Rome itself. This official division merely served to formalize the divide which had always existed in one form or another. Though Latin was the language of administration and would remain so for centuries, there were a number of distinctions between the Eastern Roman Empire and the Western Roman Empire. Owing to its location and to the fact that it was once a part of the Macedonian Empire of Alexander the Great, the Eastern Roman Empire was more developed and urbanized than its western counterpart. This afforded them greater financial power and helped spare them from many of the tribulations which quickly followed for the west.

Their greater finances allowed the Eastern Roman Empire not only to employ mercenaries at a greater rate than did the west but also to more easily buy the services of figures like Attila the Hun. These things helped secure the east against collapse during the fifth century, the way the west did. The sack of Rome in 410 CE came as a devastating blow to the entire empire, and what followed for the west was nothing short of an ending. Over the next few decades, Rome bled power and territory at a staggering rate as the Germanic Tribes, referred to in Roman texts as Barbarians, ravaged the increasingly defenseless empire.

Another factor which helped the Eastern Roman Empire fare better was the nearly impenetrable defenses of Constantinople itself. Well-positioned along the Bosporus Strait, Constantinople stood for centuries safe behind complex and well-built defenses. The walls fortified during the reign of Theodosius II in the mid-fifth century were not breached until 1204 CE. This combination of security and financial stability put the Eastern Empire in a position to weather the chaotic fifth century and emerge more or less unscathed, but this did not mean that they avoided danger altogether.

In addition to fortifying the walls of Constantinople, Theodosius II undertook a number of generally less successful measures against the Empire's foes. In 424 CE, after years of raids by the Huns, he negotiated an annual payment of three hundred and fifty pounds of gold in exchange for the Huns agreeing to end their raiding. When Attila and his brother Breda rose to prominence in 433 CE, the price was doubled to seven hundred pounds. This was a great example of both the empire's weakness and its ability to acquire funds when the need arose.

An attempt alongside the Western Roman Empire to repel a Vandal invasion of Roman North Africa in 439 CE failed utterly, but in 443 CE, when two returning armies were ambushed and destroyed by the Huns, the sudden increased danger from the Huns meant that further negotiation was needed. In a humiliating settlement, the Eastern Roman Empire agreed to increase their tribute to twenty-one hundred pounds of gold, a sixfold increase over what it had been just twenty years prior. But while this sudden increase in danger to the Eastern Roman Empire was significant, it was far from the only change they underwent during that difficult century.

By the time Attila the Hun died in 453 CE, the Byzantine Empire had already established significant contacts with a number of tribes that had come to the empire from the east. The Alans, a nomadic people originally from a region in modern Iran, had settled in such numbers and been given such power within the empire that the Alanic general Aspar came to hold great influence over three successive Eastern Roman Emperors. That the last of these three, Leo I, had had him killed in 471 CE is largely irrelevant given how common, in general, such power struggles were at the time. What mattered most was the fact that the tribes, which had devastated the western empire over the previous century, had become important enough within it in their own right to be entrusted with positions of power.

The practice of using so-called Barbarians to fend off other tribes was hardly unique to the Eastern Roman Empire, but they possessed greater capital with which to employ them. In 476 CE, when the Gothic-Roman general Odoacer deposed the final Western Roman Emperor, Romulus Augustulus, the Eastern Roman Empire was left with little choice but to work with him until he betrayed the Eastern Emperor Zeno by supporting a rival claimant. Zeno's solution to that problem came not in the form of raising Roman armies and reconquering Italy but in seeking the aid of Ostrogothic leader Theodoric the Great, to whom Zeno gave the order to kill and replace Odoacer in 493 CE.

The significance of that event is twofold. On the one hand, it demonstrated that the Eastern Roman Empire was still deeply interested in the affairs of the west, even after the Western Roman Empire had died out completely. On the other hand, it shows that though the interest was there, the power was not. In addition, although Constantinople was wealthy, it was not the military power that it needed to be if it was to support its interest in the west. Though both of these factors would change in time, with the Byzantine Empire both growing stronger and growing less interested in the Latin West, these changes, especially the latter, would take time to play out. By the end of the fifth century, the

Eastern Roman Empire was still deeply tied to the west culturally, and the golden age it would experience during the Justinian Dynasty was brought about in part because of this continued desire to hold onto tradition and the greater empire that had once existed.

Still, the ability of the Justinian Emperors to build that golden age had been possible, in part, due to the competent reign of the final Leonid Emperor Anastasius I. His reign, from 491 to 518 CE, was characterized both by stability and by financial reforms. He completed Constantine's efforts to reform the coinage of the empire by introducing a new, strictly weighted copper coin for general use. He also reformed the taxation system, doing away with the much-despised Chrysargyron Tax. His financial reforms left the empire in excellent shape, with a treasury containing over three hundred thousand pounds of gold at the time of his death. By the sixth century, the Eastern Empire was in a position to retake the western imperial holdings and possessed the clear desire to do so.

Chapter 2:
The Justinian Dynasty

The Justinian Dynasty is commonly said to have reigned over a golden age of the Byzantine Empire. Beginning with the reign of Emperor Justin I which started in 518 CE, the dynasty lasted until the death of Emperor Maurice in 602 CE. This dynasty saw the Byzantine Empire reach its greatest territorial scope. As important as that was, however, the deep cultural change that took place during the period was even more significant. When Justin I took the throne, he was largely illiterate and spoke little to no Greek. He surrounded himself with educated advisors, including his nephew and successor Justinian I, to counteract this lack. Still, the simple fact that a man who barely spoke Greek could become the Byzantine Emperor spoke of how "Latin" the empire still was. In contrast, by the time the first Emperor of the Heraclian Dynasty reigned in the early seventh century, Latin as a language was only being used ceremonially.

This transition was in part the result of the Byzantine Empire's initial success in reclaiming many of the western territories, as well as their subsequent loss of the same. At the start, however, the Justinian Dynasty benefited from relative peace and stability, which lasted until the final years of Justin's reign. The most important accomplishment of his reign was the mending of relations with the Papacy.

Justin himself was a devout Orthodox Christian which, in the sixth century, meant that he was in line with the official positions of the Papacy. Prior Eastern Roman Emperors had been Monophysites, a Christian group who disagreed with the Papacy over whether or not Jesus could be both divine and human in nature, believing that he could not have been. This dispute, known as the Acacian Schism, had been an issue for over three decades by the time Justin I and Patriarch John of Cappadocia formally ended it in 519 CE.

As significant as this was to Christendom at the time, it paled in comparison to the accomplishments of the man who succeeded Justin I: Justinian I. Justinian I was a man of great focus when it came to issues that mattered to him, but he was one who disregarded the things that did not. He cared little for class distinction, having chosen to marry a lower-class woman by the name of Theodora who had worked as an actress and a prostitute. He did this only after his uncle made it legally possible for him to do so in 525 CE, just two years before his own reign began. When he took the throne, he inherited a war with the Sassanid Empire of Persia, which had begun in the final years of his uncle's reign. When his general Belisarius suffered a defeat at the Battle of Callinicum in 531 CE, Justinian quickly took advantage of the unrelated death of the Sassanid Emperor to negotiate peace with his successor. At the cost of eleven thousand pounds of gold, Justinian signed the "Eternal Peace" agreement of 532 CE. His focus simply was not on the east but rather lay directed toward the west.

The same year that peace with the Sassanids was secured, Justinian was forced to deal with a domestic threat that nearly ended his reign then and there. The Nika Riots were a response to Justinian's habit of appointing ministers who were efficient and effective at their jobs but who were unpopular with the people. Much of life in Constantinople at the time revolved around associations known as "demes" which supported competitors in various sports, particularly chariot racing. These demes were essentially sports associations, but they operated quite differently from the ones we know in the modern day. Not only would members of demes support their faction in sporting events, that faction would also have political positions which they would often shout at the Emperor between races at the formal events. Over the years, these demes evolved into informal entities which were one part political party, one part street gang.

As one can imagine from that description, it was not uncommon for brawls to break out during sports events and for minor riots to occur as a consequence. If any murders took place, the law stated that the murderers would be hanged. In 532 CE, such an event happened, and two of the murderers—one from the blue faction and one from the green faction—happened to escape. As their respective factions demanded that they be pardoned, Justinian, who was in the midst of negotiating with the Sassanids and had raised taxes leading up to the riots, feared the possibility of chaos and commuted their sentences.

At the next race, however, this move proved not to be enough, and the formerly bitter rival factions found themselves united against the Emperor. With shouts of "Nika," meaning "victory" which gave the riots their name, they besieged the palace. Justinian, it is said, considered fleeing, but he was dissuaded by Theodora and hatched a plan instead. He sent a eunuch by the name of Narsus out with a bag of gold. He had the eunuch give gold to the leaders of the blue faction as well as a reminder that Justinian supported them—on the other hand, the man the rioters were trying to replace him with, Hypatius, supported the green faction.

This turned out to be enough to persuade them as the blue faction members quickly abandoned the green faction members who, suddenly bereft of the numbers they had enjoyed before, found themselves at the mercy of Justinian's generals. A total of thirty thousand people are said to have been killed that week, and half the city burned down, including its most prominent church the Hagia Sophia. Justinian would use this as an opportunity to rebuild the city—in particular, the Hagia Sophia—and make it his, further securing his own power through the bloodshed.

Justinian's greatest obsession lay with the west, in the lands of the former Western Roman Empire. Historians often refer to him as the "last Roman" for this reason, as much of his reign ended up dedicated to partially successful efforts to reconquer the western territories. This started with the Vandalic War, a war with a Germanic tribe called the Vandals which had taken much of Rome's territory in North Africa during the collapse of the Western Empire. It was the first and arguably most successful of Justinian's wars of reconquest. Lasting from 533-534 CE, it resulted in the crushing defeat of the Vandals and the conquest of the land. Though it was costly and it ultimately took until 548 CE to fully pacify the region, the endeavor was a success.

Contrasting this was his war to reclaim Italy which, though similarly successful in the 530s, dragged on for far longer and ended up being significantly more costly. Belisarius was again dispatched with an army, that time around with the intention to reclaim the former heartland of the Roman Empire and the city itself from the Ostrogoths. Having fallen since the days of Theoderic, the Ostrogoths of Italy under the reign of Theodahad were in a poor position to hold out against the invading Byzantines. Though it lasted longer than the Vandalic War, taking the Byzantines from 535 until 540 CE to conquer, it was initially a great victory for Justinian.

These initial victories slowly gave way to problems,

despite how much they may have appeared to be great in the beginning. For one thing, Justinian's westward focus left him vulnerable when the Sassanids broke the Eternal Peace in 540 CE. Though the Byzantines lost no territory in the sporadic fighting that occurred during the following twenty-two years, it did serve to further drain the empire's resources. When the Ostrogothic resurgence began in 541 CE, it took another thirteen years of fighting to retake and secure the Italian peninsula. In all, the campaigns were a success, and Justinian succeeded in securing territory that stretched as far as the coast of modern-day Spain. The cost, however, was tremendous.

By the end of Justinian's reign, though the borders of the Byzantine Empire had reached the greatest extent that they ever would, the treasury which had been overflowing with gold when his uncle first began his reign was empty. The empire was left overtaxed in more ways than one with its resources stretched thin and its people chaffing under the increased tax dues. The main problem that the Emperor faced during his reign was an inability to realize that his good fortune had not continued past the 530s. It would take some time before the Byzantines lost everything he had spent his reign retaking, but before terribly long, they would.

One accomplishment of Justinian's reign that lasted well beyond its inception was the Code of Justinian. Another example of Justinian's ability to focus on matters which were important to him, the code was compiled to remedy a problem he had noted in the way Roman Law was handled in the Byzantine Empire. When he came to the throne, he almost immediately ordered a compilation of imperial constitutions. Rome had existed for so long and had gone through so many often-dramatic changes in leadership that it had numerous constitutions and laws in effect, which were often handled in different ways by different courts. Justinian saw the bureaucratic mess that this resulted in and thus undertook to curb the number of court proceedings which occurred in a given year by reducing the number of constitutions.

The process itself took five years to complete, and by 534 CE, the entire code had been promulgated throughout the empire. Though initially a success and done in three parts as he had intended, Justinian, later on, discovered the need to introduce new laws. All in all, however, the project had its intended effect, and the code remained in place for centuries following his death. It was even used in the 11th century by western scholars as a source for older Roman law.

The three other Emperors of the Justinian Dynasty invariably dealt with the aftermath of Justinian's ambition. Justin II sought to continue his predecessor's successes but had neither the funds nor the talent to do so. His realization of just how dire the empire's financial situation was had led him to suspend payment to the neighboring Avars, ending a truce which had been in place for two decades. The Avars, in response, allied with the Lombards, who went on to take over nearly all of Italy outside of the major cities and Sicily. Though he succeeded in holding back the forces of the Avars, his troubles with the Sassanids in the late sixth century resulted in the loss of the vital fortress of Dara in Syria and pushed Justin II over the edge. He abdicated a broken man and was succeeded by Tiberius II.

Tiberius was a more capable Emperor, but he still faced the same central issues plaguing the empire in that period. Having started his reign in 574 CE, he had, by 579 CE, already noted that his forces were complete overextended. Though he fared well against the Avars, the Byzantine's continuing struggles against the Sassanids made it impossible to deal with them with any degree of finality. By 582 CE, there seemed to be no end in sight for the Persian conflict, and Tiberius himself was dying, having eaten food that was either poisoned or simply ill-prepared. With no son to leave the empire to, the throne passed to his primary general, Maurice, the final Emperor of the Justinian Dynasty.

Maurice enjoyed the longest reign of any Emperor in the dynasty save for Justinian himself. Despite this and the numerous military victories that he had, both before he took the throne and after, he was the only one of them who was deposed. Though he was a truly capable general, he suffered from the lack of readily available funds in the face of frequent military campaigns, just as his predecessors had been. He was the only Justinian Emperor to truly defeat the Sassanids in 591 CE, ending up with a peace deal that actually saw the Persian nation cede territory to Byzantium instead of a deal based on Byzantine tribute payments. The price of this, however, was the need to cut military wages by a quarter in 588 CE, a move which provoked a mutiny which he barely managed to quell.

By 602 CE, though he had been one of the most successful Emperors the Byzantines had had in recent decades, Maurice had become wildly unpopular. Another military coup turned out to be insurmountable, and it ended in the death of Maurice and his six sons. A military officer named Phocas was crowned Emperor, and the military moved to secure his new reign, but it came at a significant cost. The Sassanids, realizing what an opportunity the sudden instability and loss of a capable leader meant for the Byzantines, took that chance to start a war which would last for 26 years and exhaust both sides at a truly critical juncture.

Chapter 3:
The Decline of the Empire and the Rise of Islam

To understand just how disastrous Phocas' reign was for the Byzantine Empire, it is important to understand just what it represented. Though for much of its history, the Roman Empire had been subject to significant succession crises, since the fall of Rome, the Eastern Roman Empire had been relatively stable in that respect. Issues such as the Nika Riots had been quelled, and there hadn't been any major civil conflicts beyond that—other than a short problem in the fifth century between Emperor Zeno and his brother-in-law Basilicus. The deposition of Maurice and the ascent of Phocas thus represented a struggle that the empire had not experienced for decades and, as a result, had been quite ill-equipped to handle.

Maurice had defeated the Sassanids in part by helping the exiled prince Khosrow, who would become Khosrow II, to take the Persian throne. In exchange for this, the Byzantine Empire had been ceded significant territories in northeastern Mesopotamia and the Caucasus region and had its annual tribute revoked. With the death of Maurice, Khosrow had an opportunity to attack the Byzantine Empire both to avenge his old ally Maurice and to retake the territory he had only reluctantly agreed to give up in the first place. It would be the final and most devastating war between the two empires, and it would ultimately leave both exhausted and vulnerable.

The Byzantines may well have done better against the initial assaults by the Sassanids had Phocas proven himself a more competent leader. Given that he was just a centurion before he was elevated to Emperor, Phocas had no connection to the local elite, and he distrusted them completely. To get around this, he practiced nepotism on a scale beyond the norm for the period, appointing his brothers and nephew to various posts within Constantinople. Adding to this was his general paranoia. He came to believe that his position was precarious and, as a consequence, spent much of his time putting down conspiracies—both real and imagined—and purging his enemies. He devoted so much of his eight-year reign to this pursuit that his response to the Sassanids was ineffective at best.

Within six years, the Sassanid forces had come to occupy Syria, Mesopotamia, and most of Asia Minor. When Narses, a Maurice loyalist, defected, Phocas invited him to Constantinople with the promise of safety and then had him burned alive. Such conduct would have likely resulted in rebellion even if the empire hadn't been facing an existential threat in the form of the Sassanids. In this case, it came in the form of Heraclius the Elder, a powerful Exarch of Carthage; his cousin Nicetas; and his son Heraclius. They started their effort to overthrow the blatant tyrant in 609 CE by cutting off the supply of grain to Constantinople while they assembled their army and navy. The following year, through invading by land and sea, they seized the city after a two-day siege, executed Phocas, and had Heraclius crowned Emperor.

Immediately after Heraclius took the throne, the Sassanids enjoyed their greatest victories. The ancient cities of Damascus and Jerusalem fell to the Persian forces in 613 CE, and the True Cross, the cross said to have been used in the Crucifixion of Jesus Christ was stolen. With one of the holiest cities in the Christian tradition occupied and possibly the religion's holiest relic taken back to the Sassanid capital of Ctesiphon, Heraclius' response took on the form of a Holy

War. Before he could start his counteroffensive in earnest, however, Heraclius was left with the difficult task of reorganizing a severely weakened empire.

With the Sassanids having taken the Levant and Egypt, the Byzantine Empire was left without much of its usual grain supply. It also lost significant tax revenue due to the loss of the provinces. To deal with this crisis, Heraclius imposed severe budget cuts on the entire administration, halving the pay of government officials and enforcing extreme fines on anyone who committed acts of corruption. He also devalued the currency, ordering the creation of lighter coins to ease the financial burden of the state. While in other times, such actions may well have sparked a rebellion against the government, the loss of Jerusalem and the holy relics had created in the people of the Byzantine Empire a religious fervor which made them more than willing to put up with such discomfort if it meant dealing with the Persians.

Heraclius' counteroffensive began in 622 CE, with his armies marching across Anatolia to push out the occupying Persians. The Chronicles are unclear as to what truly transpired, but what is known is that in the autumn of 622 CE, he won a decisive victory over the Sassanid general Shahrbaraz in eastern Anatolia. This served to push the Persian forces out of the region and give the empire temporary relief.

Though Heraclius offered peace to Khosrow in 624 CE, his offer was rejected, and he ended up invading Persia. Traveling through the Caucasus region, he chose to spend the winter in Caucasian Albania in the east of the region to gather more troops and be ready to assault the Persian mainland in the spring. Khosrow sent multiple armies after him in that region, but as fortified as Heraclius' position was and as capable as he was as a general, they made little progress. Shahrbaraz, in particular, fared poorly when, following the infiltration of two supposed deserters from Heraclius' camp, he was led to believe that Heraclius was attempting to flee. Sending half his forces to the position where the fraudulent traitors had said that he was moving toward, he soon found himself ambushed instead. With his army destroyed, Shahrbaraz, according to the accounts of the time, barely managed to flee, leaving behind his troops, his resources, and apparently his clothing

With his enemy's primary general naked and alone, fleeing to the nearest Persian fortress, Heraclius managed to secure his position farther in, spending the rest of the winter in Trebizond. While Heraclius kept his forces in the Caucasus region and northern Persia, Khosrow sought to force him to pull back by sending his armies around his foe to assault Constantinople itself. Allying with the Turkish Avars, his generals sought to attempt a two-pronged siege of the city from both the European side and through crossing the Bosporus Strait. This siege in 626 CE ultimately failed, however, owing to the city's notorious defenses and the Byzantine navy's complete control of the Aegean sea, Bosporus Strait, and Sea of Marmara.

While Heraclius did divert some of his forces to the city to reinforce it, he was left with more than enough troops to raid the Persian heartland. The Persian raids culminated with the Battle of Ninevah. As he returned home, having devastated most of the Persian armies, he encountered an army under the command of the Sassanid commander Rhahzadh near the ruins of Ninevah. The battle was a bloody affair with an estimated six thousand Sassanid troops dying alongside their commander. It was a significant victory for the Byzantines as it left the Persians with no viable armies left to throw against the Byzantines. What remained of the Persian forces overthrew Khosrow and replaced him with his son Kavadh II.

With a new Sassanid leader to negotiate with, Heraclius offered a deal which saw the restoration of the lost Byzantine territory and the True Cross in exchange for no harsh penalties being issued against the defeated power. In truth, each side was virtually as exhausted as the other, and Heraclius had no desire to press his luck. With the deal agreed to, the two sides left to lick their wounds, each unaware that they would not get much of a chance.

Happening almost in complete chronological parallel to the final Byzantine-Sassanid War was Muhammad's rise to power and subsequent death. Though the prophet of Islam never expanded his territory past the Arabian Peninsula, the same could not be said of his successors. The Rashidun Caliphate, the name given at the time to the first four Caliphs following Muhammad's death in 632 CE, had overseen a quarter century of near-constant expansion at an incredible rate. Whether one wants to call it luck, divine providence, or serendipity, the fact that the Arabs began their expansion at the exact same time when their most powerful neighbors had just finished destroying one another certainly turned out to be favorable for them. By the end of Rashidun Caliphate in 661 CE, their territory already spanned from modern Tunisia to modern Afghanistan.

For the Byzantines, this meant the immediate loss of Egypt, much of North Africa, the Levant, and Mesopotamia, as these found themselves completely unable to withstand the frequent raids by the battle-hardened and well-supplied Arab armies. In this, the seventh century was for the Byzantines one characterized by terrible tribulation and change. They went from being an empire which spanned from Iberia to the Levant to one which was confined to Anatolia, the Balkans, and fragments of Italy. This brought with it a number of social changes as well.

In particular, the Byzantine Empire quickly ruralized as the loss of grain-producing regions such as Egypt made supplying large cities impossible. The same thing happened in the Western Roman Empire over the course of the fifth century as the collapse of the old trade routes forced people to abandon the cities. This, in turn, forced the Byzantine Empire to make the transition from a Late Antique empire to a Medieval state.

Historians argue that another consequence of this transition marks the moment when it is more correct to classify the Byzantine Empire as a successor state, such as those which developed in the west, rather than a continuation of Rome itself. Given how much Roman territory they lost, one could make that argument on those grounds alone, but it goes beyond that. Heraclius was the Emperor who introduced Greek as the official language of the empire. Considering that among the Emperors of the previous dynasty, only Maurice had been a native Greek speaker, that was an enormous change to make, and yet it happened. It speaks to a growing distance between Constantinople and their Latin Roman roots, even as they would continue to claim their status as Rome's continuation right until the end.

One aspect of the growing cultural split between the east and the west was the position that the Eastern Church would take on the issue of icons. Iconoclasm is the banning of religious icons for fear that using them in moments of worship can lead to worship of the icons themselves rather than of God. Beginning during the reign of Leo III of the Isaurian Dynasty, the practice of tearing down religious icons became official policy in 730 CE. The Western Church disagreed with them so strongly about the issue of iconoclasm that it influenced their decision to distance themselves from Constantinople.

The Byzantine Papacy refers to the period 537 to 752 CE wherein the Papacy in Rome required the approval of the Emperor for the appointment of new Popes. This was the result of Justinian I choosing to appoint three Popes over the course of his reign following the conquest of Italy from the Ostrogoths. The Papacy put up with this with very little complaint because they had been, for a time, happy to be closer to the continued Roman Empire. The issue of Iconoclasm was one of the few major differences between them at that point in history—few people in the west opposed icons, and the papacy itself was very much in favor of them. By 752 CE, the Papacy and Constantinople were very much divided due to numerous factors.

The Muslim Conquests took up much of Constantinople's time and energy, diverting their attention away from Italy where the Lombards grew increasingly powerful and threatening to Rome. By the turn of the century, the Papacy had approved a new Emperor in the west for the first time in over three centuries, and Charlemagne and his successors became for Rome far more favorable option than the Emperors in the east.

Chapter 4: Resurgence Under the Macedonian Dynasty

Though the Byzantine Empire reached its territorial zenith under Justinian I, it reached its true peak in terms of power under the Macedonian Dynasty. Under the Reign of Basil I and his dynastic successors, it grew to once again become a force to be reckoned with in the eastern Mediterranean. In what some have termed the Macedonian Renaissance, its culture thrived as well, with education reviving and ancient texts being copied for distribution to the growing cities.

By mid-ninth century, the Byzantine Empire had changed its administrative structure significantly. With the loss of territory during the initial Muslim Conquests, the old trade system had been disrupted, and while this mostly resulted in the decline of the cities in the beginning, it also resulted in the reorganization of the provincial system. In place of the provinces which had been the administrative divisions put in place by Constantine and Diocletian, the Theme System of military administration took form. It was similar in a way to the feudal system of western Europe which developed after the fall of Rome, as the land was divided into plots used by soldiers and their families in exchange for service. The primary difference was that the land remained under the control of the Imperium, and the Emperor could and often did remove and appoint administrators at will.

It was from this system that Basil I emerged as a simple peasant before climbing his way up the ranks under the reign of Michael III. When he took power himself in 867

CE, he quickly proved himself to be a capable—if mildly unstable—ruler. Though he warred successfully against the Paulicians and the Arabs, managing to briefly retake the island of Cyprus, most of Sicily was lost during his reign. His foreign policy, though ambitious and often westward-focused, was not the most notable part of his reign: where he truly shined as a leader was on the domestic front, and he came to be known as the second Justinian for his legislative work. The collection of laws he compiled came to be known as the Basilika, a collection of sixty books. It was the most extensive legal project undertaken since the reign of Justinian I.

The religious tension between Constantinople and Rome was one thing that Basil attempted to remedy. His solution was to exile the then-Patriarch of Constantinople Photios and to replace him with Ignatius, whom Rome favored, to curry favor with them without giving up much ground. This, however, backfired—ten years later, in 877 CE, Ignatius died and was replaced again by Photios. Photios' reclamation of his post resulted in an informal but undeniable split between the churches in the east and west, which helped pave the way for the eventual formal split in the 11th century.

Under Basil's reign, a culture of letters formed throughout the empire, and educated men began writing to each other to spread ideas and consult with one another; this is similar to the culture which developed during the later, more famous Renaissance. Though this cultural flowering continued during the reigns of Basil's immediate successors, his already limited military successes did not. Under the reign of Basil I, Boris I of Bulgaria had allied the church in his country with Constantinople instead of Rome. While this had been a boon for Basil, it quickly became clear in the years and decades following his death that the Bulgarians had no interest in being subservient to the Byzantines.

Under Simeon I, the Bulgarians waged two wars against the Byzantines, first in 894-896 CE, and then again in 913-927 CE. Both were successes for Simeon, with the first gaining them the Bulgarian kingdom territory in Thrace and the second gaining Simeon himself very reluctant recognition as a fellow Emperor by Constantinople. The situation with the Bulgarians would not change until the final quarter of the century, and the tribute payments that the Byzantines were forced to pay put a drain on their coffers.

The situation with the Arabs had become far more stable by the beginning of the Macedonian Dynasty with an uneasy status quo setting in, which was not dissimilar to that which they had experienced with the Sassanid Persians in earlier centuries. Unlike the situation with Sassanids, the Byzantines were not crushed underfoot by the conquering Muslims under the initial assaults, but they were weakened greatly. As both sides settled into a pattern of launching raids against the other and then retaliating in kind, the Byzantines managed not to lose further significant territory to them until after this dynasty was finished.

A significant development came in the form of the newly emerged state of Kievan Rus in the ninth century. While it was initially yet another rival with which to war against, Kievan Rus, following its Christianization traditionally said to have occurred in 987 CE, became an ally of sorts and trading partner to the Byzantines. Though they fought repeatedly, often over the desire in Kiev to establish more favorable trade agreements, the Byzantines ended up holding a great deal of influence over the comparatively fledgling state. Their architectural style came to dominate in Kiev, their style of writing greatly influenced that of the

Kievan elite, and their trade ties significantly helped to build up the eastern European polity.

One thing which greatly influenced their success in the next century was the shift in policy on the issue of Iconoclasm. While it had been woefully unpopular with Rome, that hadn't been the worst aspect of following the policy that they did for much of the eighth and ninth centuries. The cultural cost of Iconoclasm was immense as the policy called not just to ban people from worshiping with icons but for the icons themselves to be destroyed. Numerous works of Byzantine art were destroyed over the course of the period, with the policy remaining in place first from 730-783 CE and again from 814-842 CE. Curiously, in both instances, it was a Queen Regent ruling on behalf of a king still in his minority that ended it. The second time, under the regency of Queen Theodora, mother of Michael III, it was ended for good. During the reigns of both Michael III and Basil I, the people were free to create religious artwork again, contributing to the renaissance which had fed the period's revival.

The true height of the Macedonian period came under the reign of Basil II. Ruling from 976-1025 CE, Basil proved himself to be both a capable administrator and a ruthless general. As his father Romanos II died in 963 CE when Basil was only five years old, he was left unable to rule. Under the regencies of the general Nikephoros II and his nephew John I Tzimiskes, the pair became successive co-Emperors to the child. It was not until 976 CE that Basil came to rule alone, and by that point, the incompetence and administrative neglect of his co-Emperors had left the empire in a state of severe civil unrest. The wealthy Anatolian generals Bardas Skleros and Bardas Phokas both took up arms against the new Emperor, seeking to reduce him back to the powerless figurehead he had been under the reigns of Nikephoros II and John I.

Phokas was at first loyal to the new Emperor and served to help him put down Skleros' rebellion in 979 CE. When he, in turn, chose to rebel in 989 CE, however, his old enemy became his ally against Basil. In need of more allies, Basil entered negotiations with Vladimir I of Kievan Rus, who agreed to supply troops and supplies to the embattled Emperor and even convert both himself and his nation to Christianity in exchange for Basil's sister Anna's hand in marriage. This was an unprecedented move as the Byzantines, in true Roman fashion, had continued to see the various peoples of Europe outside their own domain as "barbarians." As his situation required sacrifice, however, Basil agreed, and after Phokas and Skleros had been dealt with in 989 CE, the promised pair were wed.

Beginning his reign under such unfavorable conditions had a profound impact on the still-young ruler, and advice apparently given by his old enemy seemed to have just as important an influence on Basil. According to the historian Psellus, after he was defeated, Bardas Skleros is said to have imparted on the young Basil the following:

> *"Cut down the governors who become over-proud. Let no generals on campaign have too many resources. Exhaust them with unjust exactions, to keep them busied with their own affairs. Admit no woman to the imperial councils. Be accessible to no one. Share with few your most intimate plans."*

Once the civil wars were finished, Basil II found himself needing to address a matter which had been impossible to see to since they began: the empire's external enemies. The Fatamid Dynasty had taken full advantage of its enemy's internal strife and had seized back lands in Anatolia which Nikephoros II and John I had managed to reclaim. Over the next decade, Basil was forced to take to the field personally on numerous occasions against the Fatimids, initially in defense against the Emirate of Aleppo. Though neither side proved capable of achieving a decisive blow against the other, Basil held his own against the Muslim forces well enough that he managed to attain a lasting peace with them in 1000 CE. This secured his eastern front for the rest of his reign and allowed him time to focus on an issue which mattered far more to him: the Bulgarians.

Throughout Basil's reign, though he enjoyed great victories against the Georgians and the Khazars, no one was as devastated by the warrior Emperor than the Bulgarians. Earning himself the nickname "the Bulgar Slayer," Basil II managed to undertake an utterly crushing campaign against the Bulgarian Empire. While Basil was occupied with his civil wars and his wars in the east, Tsar Samuel of Bulgaria took advantage of the opportunity and conducted raids throughout Byzantine lands. Basil, having no desire to leave such a capable enemy so close to his European holdings, set out in 1000 CE with a force fit to raid and capture Bulgarian-held towns and fortresses. For the next eighteen years, he continued this pattern annually, slowly chipping away at the Bulgarian lands until they were ultimately all in his possession.

One particularly violent scenario from the war paints a picture of just how brutal Basil had become by the end of his reign. In 1014 CE, Basil and his general Nikephoros

Xiphias routed and surrounded a Bulgarian army, capturing fifteen thousand men. The chronicles say that in his cruelty, he had ninety-nine out of every hundred men blinded, and left the final one with only one eye to lead the others home. The story went on that when Tsar Samuel saw the sight of his utterly destroyed army, it resulted in a stroke which killed him. Now, regardless of whether or not this is exaggerated, what is known for certain is that by the end of the Conquest of Bulgaria, Basil was so widely feared that Bulgaria's ally Croatia decided to accept his supremacy in the area for fear of facing his wrath if they did not.

Whether one sees him as a brutal butcher, a brilliant tactician, or both, what is certain is that by the end of Basil's reign in 1025 CE, the Byzantine Empire was at its absolute zenith in terms of power. Unlike the state, it was in at the end of the reign of Justinian I, its forces and resources were not overextended, and it had the power to hold onto what he had gained. He even left the treasury full of gold, a rarity for any wartime leader, let alone one who campaigned as frequently and enthusiastically as did Basil II. His reign was a good one, and he might well have been the most capable leader that the Empire ever had. But while the state of affairs in the Byzantine Empire was good when he died, that did not last long.

Chapter 5:
The Crusades and Their Impact

There is no shortage out there of books on the Crusades, as the subject has fascinated people throughout the west for centuries. Most of these, however, tend to focus on the crusades from the perspective of the Western Frankish forces who responded to the Papal call to arms. What is given somewhat less emphasis is the role played by the Byzantines both during the calls for help in the first place and during the conflicts themselves. To understand how the Byzantine Empire went from a position of strength in 1025 CE to needing to call for help in 1095 CE would require some explanation.

Basil II left the Byzantine Empire in the best shape it had ever been in after the fall of Rome. His brother Constantine VIII, who had technically been co-Emperor with him since they were so-named in 962 CE, had remained in the shadows, far away from governance due to a personal lack of interest in the concept. This lack of interest did not change after his brother's death, and since Basil died childless, his brother assumed the throne for the last three years of his own life. Constantine VIII was by all accounts a negligent and sadistic ruler whose brief reign is generally understood to have been a catastrophe. On his deathbed, with no son to pass the throne to, he attempted to give it to Constantine Dalessenus, a powerful aristocrat, by marrying the man to his daughter Zoe. He was then persuaded by court officials, who preferred a more easily controlled Emperor, to marry her instead to Romanos Argyros—it was he who succeeded Constantine VIII as Romanos III.

Romanos III reigned for six years, which ended when

he died in what is generally assumed to have been an act of murder. He was then replaced by Michael IV, Empress Zoe's lover, who was in turn succeeded by his nephew Michael V whom Zoe adopted. She remained in power from 1028 CE until 1042 CE when Michael V tried to exile her. It resulted to a popular uprising took which removed him from power in Zoe's favor. She remained in power until her death in 1050 CE. Having married again, she was succeeded by her final husband, Constantine IX.

In all this time, none of the Empire's rulers came close to possessing her uncle's skill at administration or military matters, and through the decades of instability and intrigue, the running of the state ended in large part in the hands of civil servants who understood little of the task given them. The single biggest victim of this period was the Byzantine army, which had been exceptionally strong under Basil II, a man who was himself far too feared by the end of his reign to have any reason to fear his army. But the weak rulers of this period did fear the potential in the army for insurrection; thus, they decided to retire their remaining native troops and began to rely entirely on mercenaries.

In this time, they faced renewed troubles from Bulgarian rebels, the new incursions of the Normans who were beginning to strike against both Byzantine territory in Southern Italy and the Emirate of Sicily, and the Seljuk Turks in the east. Though they held off these threats for a time, by the 1090s, the Turks and Normans, in particular, were enjoying success against the weary and weakened Byzantines.

Worsening their position was the fact that by the mid-11th century, the schism between the churches in the west and the churches in the east was complete. What was truly a slow-building dispute between the two sides came to a head in 1054 CE. There were numerous doctrinal disputes at the heart of the schism, most notably a dispute over the wording of the Nicene Creed, an important statement of belief used in both eastern and western liturgy. At the heart of the schism, however, was an increasing and mutual resentment on both sides for the other's claim to authority. This divide had been building since the end of the Byzantine Papacy in 752 CE and became more formal following the mutual excommunications of Pope Leo IX and Patriarch Michael I Cerularius. Even in the face of the Norman invasion of southern Italy which threatened Constantinople and Rome, the two sides could not come together to find a solution.

The 1071 CE Battle of Manzikert was a crushing defeat for the Byzantines and marked the first time in their history that a Byzantine Emperor, Romanos IV, was captured by a Muslim commander. It lost them significant control and power over Anatolia and pushed them back further than they had been in decades. Twenty years later, under Emperor Alexios I, the Byzantines won a brutal victory at the Battle of Levounion but were left in a vexing position. With the death of Robert Guiscard of the Normans in 1085 CE and the death of the Turkish Sultan the next year, that victory should have put Alexios I in a position to retake significant lost land. Unfortunately, he lacked the troops to accomplish that task. Seventy years of bureaucratic incompetence had left the Byzantine Empire's defenses in tatters. Though Alexios did work to rebuild the Byzantine army, it did not progress quickly enough to match his desires.

In a position to strike against his enemy but needing allies desperately, Alexios turned to Rome. Alexios knew how formidable the soldiers in the west could be from the Byzantine's encounters with the Normans in Italy. Hoping to capitalize on that, he sent ambassadors to request aid from the western kingdoms. At the Council Piacenza in 1095 CE, his ambassadors managed to make their appeal, and it ended up being more successful than he ever dreamed or wanted. The council had been called at the end of a tour through Italy and France conducted by Pope Urban II to reassert his authority after a drawn-out conflict with the Holy Roman Emperor Henry IV over which of the two had the right to appoint local church officials.

Due to the importance of the council, it was quite well-attended, needing to be held outside the city of Piacenza because two hundred bishops, four thousand church officials, and thirty thousand laymen were in attendance. When Alexios' ambassadors made their plea to help, emphasizing the suffering of Eastern Christians at the hands of the Turks, it moved their listeners, none more so than the Pope himself. Urban II urged all who were present to aid the Byzantines however way they could.

That same year, Urban II called the Council of Clermont in France and begged all who attended to do their part in striking against the infidels in the formerly Christian lands. The response was immense and well beyond the scope of anything that Alexios had likely had in mind when he first called for aid. Rather than a small disciplined mercenary army, he gained the help of thousands of undisciplined zealots, each seeking more to strike against the enemy than to follow the direction of Constantinople. That the first of these armies, a ragtag group led by the priest Peter the Hermit in 1096 CE, had been led to their slaughter in Nicaea was a perfect example of this.

When the armies led by experienced commanders arrived, they were more useful than Peter's force but no more willing to work for the Byzantine Emperor. Led by Godfrey of Boullion, the crusaders were sent by Alexios into Asia, along with a promise of provisions in exchange for oaths of loyalty. Though he did reclaim numerous cities along the Mediterranean coast through their efforts, the Crusaders came to see their oaths as having been made invalid by the fact that Alexios did not fight alongside them, particularly in their siege of Antioch.

Though the Byzantine Empire did regain most of western Anatolia, the Crusader's conquests in the Levant were taken by the princes and turned into the Levantine Crusader States. These were private kingdoms carved out of the Christian Holy Land which were to be administrated as Latin Rite states, opposing both the eastern Christians and the Muslims in the region. That most of the crusaders returned home after the crusade was finished in 1099 CE meant that these states were left vulnerable and arguably doomed to fail.

For his part, Alexios was left regretful for having called in the western soldiers in the first place. The First Crusade was an overwhelming success for much the same reason that the initial Muslim Conquests had been: the Muslim forces in the area, due in this case to division and infighting, were exhausted and ill-prepared for a well-executed military campaign when they first arrived. Over just three years, the Crusaders managed to take back more land than Christendom as a whole had held in the area in centuries. What this meant was that, though the Crusaders had accomplished all that they did and left, the fighting was certain to become significantly less one-sided once the Muslims in the area, particularly the Turks, managed to reorganize themselves. This is what happened leading up to the Second Crusade, as the reorganized Turks launched their counter-attack.

Though the First Crusade's ending was not ideal for

the Byzantines, it still gave the weary empire room to breathe and recover. One could argue that internal incompetence had done more damage to the Byzantine Empire in the 11th century than had the Turks, and it was fortunate for them that they managed to avoid such problems for decades after the First Crusade. Alexios I was succeeded in 1118 CE by his son John II. John was a leader so bizarrely pious and good-tempered by Byzantine standards that he came to be known as John the Good. It was recorded that never once during his reign did he have anyone executed or blinded, and it was not for a lack of opportunity what with him having reigned for twenty-five years. He has been referred to as the Byzantine Marcus Aurelius, and not without reason. His reign was characterized by social revival and military accomplishment, with territories lost due to the Battle of Manzikert being reclaimed and garrisoned. He left the empire in 1143 CE with a full treasury and the prospect of a bright future. As was often the case with the Byzantine Empire, however, this was not to last.

Manuel, I reigned from 1143-1180 CE in what was arguably the final good period of the Byzantine Empire. His accomplishments were few and, as with many Byzantine Emperors, his ambition far exceeded his ability. He was unsuccessful in reclaiming southern Italy or the Anatolian interior, as he attempted. What he did succeed in doing, however, was weathering the Second Crusade. The Turks struck back against the Christian states in 1144 CE, decades after their defeat in the First Crusade, and captured the county of Edessa in eastern Anatolia. In response, the Crusaders launched the Second Crusade in 1147 CE. Unlike the first Crusade, they were not facing disorganized and war-weary armies, and the difference in the results was noteworthy.

The Second Crusade was a decisive victory for the Muslims who held onto Edessa and managed to get a peace treaty with the Byzantines, securing the territorial change. It set up the Fall of Jerusalem in 1187 CE, which would result in the Third Crusade that would end in much the same way. The Third Crusade would occur from 1189-1192 CE. It would see the Crusaders retake much of the Levantine coast as well as capture the island of Cyprus but fall short of their ultimate goal of reclaiming Jerusalem. In both cases, the two Christian groups came to feel as though the other had failed them, worsening relations. In truth, both defeats were the result of the growing divide caused by the East-West Schism and the continuing political tensions between the rival powers in the region. The worsening of relations between the Byzantines and the Latin states would result in easily the most cataclysmic event in the empire's history.

Chapter 6: The Fourth Crusade

In history, you can find examples of unforced errors, unfortunate miscalculations, and unmitigated catastrophes which continue to perplex and mystify people to the present times. The Fourth Crusade, one of the last ones, was without a doubt the most unfortunate moment for the Byzantine Empire in its history, save for its final collapse. Though it was ultimately the Latin Crusaders who dealt the grievous blow to the Byzantine Empire, the empire itself was far from blameless for the position that they found themselves in.

When Manuel I died in 1180 CE, his eleven-year-old son Alexios II was left in power under the regency of his mother Maria of Antioch. Maria was of Frankish background and was unpopular as a consequence given the general sentiments toward the Latin west in Constantinople in the late 12th century. Alexios himself was but a boy and incapable of ruling on his own. Thus, his uncle Andronikos, in 1182 CE, led a popular uprising against Maria and installed himself as co-Emperor. During this uprising, he also led the Massacre of the Latins, wherein the city's thousands of Latin inhabitants were slaughtered almost to a man. The westerners in the city had grown wealthy, and jealousy was quite likely a factor in the brutal act. The strain this placed on relations with the west was both considerable and unsurprising.

Andronikos then went farther in 1183 CE by having the child Emperor strangled and marrying his twelve-year-old betrothed Agnes of France. The nobility in the Byzantine Empire had grown more powerful under the rule of Manuel I and, fearing their strength, Andronikos sought to suppress their power. His measures were characteristically brutal as he sought to wipe out anyone who might be powerful enough to try to take the throne from him. In 1185 CE, he ordered that all prisoners and their families be executed for the crime of colluding with foreign invaders, leading to a number of riots.

Amidst all of this, William II of Sicily decided to take advantage of the chaos and invade the Byzantine territory, capturing and pillaging the city of Thessalonica. When Andronikos sailed out to prevent the Normans from making further gains in his territory, Issac Angelos, the son of a military leader in Anatolia, killed Andronikos' lieutenant Stephen Hagiochristophorites and pleaded with the people of Constantinople to help him end the madness. Andronikos returned to the city to find that Issac II had been proclaimed Emperor, and though he did try to flee, he was captured and given to an angry mob who, according to accounts from the time, tore him apart.

Issac II reigned for ten years, at the end of which he was deposed and blinded by his older brother Alexios III. It was a Byzantine Empire in this state of disunion and chaos which the Crusaders found when the Fourth Crusade began.

The Third Crusade was more successful for the Crusaders than the Second Crusade had been, but as with the Second Crusade, it failed to achieve its primary goal. In the case of the Third Crusade, that goal had been the reclamation of Jerusalem which had fallen to the forces of Saladin in 1187 CE. That desire to recapture the heart of the Holy Land was still strong in 1198 CE, just six years after the end of the Third Crusade when Pope Innocent III first called for a new Crusade. Innocent III had ascended to the Papacy earlier that same year and was eager to renew the fight for Christendom.

There were a few key differences right from the start between this Crusade and those which had preceded it. For one thing, it had been less than a decade since the forces of Europe had gone to war with the Muslims, and fatigue was still quite prevalent across the continent. It was largely due to this that when Innocent III issued his Papal Bull *Post miserabile* in 1198 CE, it went almost entirely ignored. Another possible factor for this was the changing attitudes in the west toward the Greek Christians. The Crusades had brought the two sides closer together than they had been for centuries, and there was precious little that was lost in cultural translation. The Byzantines, having been forced to deal directly with the Muslim powers on their virtual doorstep, had been forced to negotiate with them from time to time. The Latin Christians, who had enjoyed the luxury of distance and did not understand this, saw the willingness to treat with their religious enemy as a betrayal of the faith. The Massacre of the Latins just a few years prior had also done little to improve the image of the Byzantines in their eyes.

Fulk of Neuilly, a popular French preacher, managed through his sermons in 1099 CE to convince Count Thibaut of Champagne to organize a tournament meant to shore up support for Innocent's crusade. He did so, and with enough support gathered for the venture, it was decided that they would avoid having to cross all the way through the Byzantine Empire and Anatolia by sailing instead to Egypt. A strike against Jerusalem from the south, they figured, would give them a strategic advantage. To that end, it was decided to approach the Venetians for the commissioning of a fleet, and Thibault was elected leader of the Crusade. When he died two years later, the leadership role was taken over by Boniface of Montferrat.

The Venetians were reluctant to get involved, but by

1201 CE, they had been persuaded to create a fleet capable of transporting thirty-three thousand, five hundred troops to Egypt for a cost of eighty-five thousand silver marks. When the crusaders arrived a year later with only twelve thousand troops and only thirty-five thousand silver marks, the Venetians threatened to keep the fleet, but they could ill-afford to do so given the vast cost of creating it. When the Doge of Venice, Enrico Dandolo, suggested that the Crusaders pay off their debt by besieging the city of Zara, some refused to do so and left, but the bulk of the army agreed to the terms.

Zara was a Catholic city which had been under the dominion of Venice for many years but had, in 1181 CE, rebelled and joined King Emeric of Hungary and Croatia in an alliance. Hungary too was a Catholic kingdom, and so, the Fourth Crusade began not by attacking a Muslim port or even a Byzantine port but one belonging to a fellow Latin Christian state. The siege did not last long with the Crusaders arriving by the 11th of November 1202 CE and entering the city by the 24th. The pillaging which followed horrified Innocent III who sent a letter threatening to excommunicate the entire army if they did not make their way to Jerusalem immediately. The leaders of the Crusade, however, not wanting to negatively impact morale, neglected to share that information.

While the Crusaders were in Zara, Boniface of Montferrat, having managed to slip away before the fleet left Venice, decided to visit his cousin, Philip of Swabia. Philip happened to be hosting Alexios Angelos, the son of the recently deposed Issac II of the Byzantine Empire. While there, Alexios promised to cover the debt owed to the Venetians, give an additional two hundred thousand silver marks to the crusaders, send ten thousand Byzantine professional troops to assist with the Crusade, and place the Eastern Church under Papal authority if they would help overthrow Alexios III and restore his father to the throne. Boniface was more than happy to relay this information to his fellow Crusaders who, in turn, found it an impossibly tempting offer. Though already having angered the Pope by attacking a Christian city, Alexios' offer turned out to be too good to turn down even with the possibility of Innocent's wrath.

The siege began on July 11th of 1203 CE, with the Venetian fleet having managed to cross the Bosporus Strait with relative ease. As the Venetian army retreated behind their walls, the Venetian siege weapons managed to start a fire which spread through one hundred and twenty acres of the city. As Alexios III rushed out to meet them, his army outnumbered them by more than two to one. The surprise attack and raging fire stole his nerve, however, and the entire army retreated back behind the walls. Disgraced and seeking a way out, Alexios had his loyalists seize as much gold as they could and fled the city. As the city officials realized what had happened, they moved quickly to depose Alexios formally and restored Issac II to the throne. The Crusaders were left in a quandary in that they had achieved their goals but realized that the man who had made them such tempting promises was not sitting on the throne. They refused to accept Issac's rule unless his son was named co-Emperor as Alexios IV and the officials, wanting the siege to end, agreed.

Upon taking power, Alexios quickly realized that there was little to no way for him to keep his promises. For one thing, Alexios III had taken around one thousand pounds of gold and jewels with him when he fled the city, and even if he had not, he had still spent the last eight years spending the empire into the ground. As he turned to destroying icons to salvage the gold in the hopes of paying the Latin army off with them, the people quickly turned on him. Within the year, he was killed and replaced by a courier named Alexios Doukas—who took the reign name Alexios V—and was quickly followed by his father who died of natural causes. The Crusaders were incensed at the death of their would-be patron and quickly moved to take what they felt they were owed by force.

The Sack of Constantinople in 1204 CE occurred on April 13th of that year and lasted for three days. The pillaging is said to have gained for the Crusaders over nine hundred thousand silver marks' worth of treasure, and they burned and looted with reckless abandon. It is said that they even seated a prostitute on the throne of the Orthodox Patriarch as a particular attack on the Greek Orthodox Church. When Innocent III heard of it, he was horrified and rebuked them in no uncertain terms, but there was little that he could do. The Byzantine Empire had fallen, and in its place, the Crusaders raised the Latin Empire.

The Latin Empire was an attempt to supplant the Byzantine Empire as the Roman Empire in the east, with the hope being that under the rule of Roman Catholics, it would in time become a Catholic state. It was ill-conceived from the start and, in the end, only lasted until 1261 CE. In a way, the eventually successful Byzantines had their old enemy the Bulgarians to thank for the ability to take the empire back from the Latins, as they warred with the Latin Empire constantly in the hopes of securing their own gains. In addition, the Empire of Nicaea formed by Byzantine nobles following the capture of Constantinople from their old territory in western Anatolia continued to raid the rump state throughout the decades following its creation. By 1250 CE, the Niceans had taken almost all of the territory surrounding the city back, and over the next eleven years and after numerous attempts, they managed to break down the resolve of the defenders. In 1261 CE, the city fell again to the people who had ruled it for nearly a thousand years. But though they had managed to take back their city, there was little that could be done to truly restore their old empire.

Chapter 7:
The Decline of the Empire and the Fall of Constantinople

The devastation caused in 1204 CE had a long-term and ultimately fatal impact on the Byzantine Empire. Even after retaking the city in 1261 CE, the Byzantines found themselves in a permanent state of decline which was only worsened by the infighting which came to define the 14th century. Worse than this was the fact that by the end of the 13th century, the Byzantine Empire found itself not only reduced to the smallest state it had ever been in but also surrounded by increasingly powerful enemies.

In the absence of a strong power based in Constantinople, the Serbians began to assert themselves in the Balkan region. The Kingdom of Serbia first emerged in 1217 CE, more than a decade after Constantinople fell. At its peak, during the Serbian imperial period under Stefan IV Dusan, it spanned much of modern-day Serbia, Montenegro, Greece, and Albania, having taken much of what was known to the Byzantines as the region of Epirus from the empire while it was under Latin occupation. By the end of Stefan's reign in 1355 CE, they also held much of formerly Byzantine Macedonia, depriving the once-powerful empire of land which held major cultural and economic significance to them.

The Bulgarians also reasserted themselves in this era, managing to reclaim much of the territory they had once held before their conquest at the hands of Basil II. The Second Bulgarian Empire came to be in 1185 CE, during the disastrous reign of Andronikos I and before the Fourth Crusade. Despite this, it was not until after their victory in the 1205 CE Battle of Adrianople over the Latin Empire that they began to reclaim their status as a regional power. At their peak, during the reign of Ivan Asen II in the early to mid-13th century, their territory spanned from the Black Sea coast of modern Bulgaria and Romania through to Macedonia. Conflicts with their neighboring states and internal strife would halt their advance, but in the end, as was the case with Serbia and eventually the Byzantine Empire as well, what truly caused the decline of Bulgaria was the rise of the most consequential regional power of the day, the Ottoman Turks.

The Seljuk Turks, united under the Sultanate of Rum, had been the primary Turkish power in Anatolia for over two centuries when the Ottomans first rose to prominence in 1299 CE. They were the primary power in the region that the Crusaders had fought against and with whom the Byzantines had signed a treaty with at the end of the Second Crusade. By the end of the 13th century, however, they were undeniably in decline. The fact that they failed to take full advantage of the chaos caused by the brief Latin Empire was proof enough of that. The Ottomans, however, starting under their first leader Osman I, grew rapidly from a small and insignificant Emirate to the most powerful Muslim state in the world. Little is known of Osman himself as Ottoman records at the time were not extensive. His son Orhan, however, was the Sultan who captured the city of Bursa in Modern Turkey, the emirate's first major capital.

Over the course of the 14th century, the Ottomans managed to capture much of Anatolia and the Balkans, so much so that by the turn of the 15th century, the Byzantine empire was surrounded on all sides. Their advance into Europe was made possible by their capture of Gallipoli in 1354 CE. This victory was made easy for them by an earthquake which struck that year, devastating the local fort in the region. With the Byzantines tied up in their own internal struggles at the time, they were unable to refortify in time to prevent the Ottomans from gaining their bridge into Europe. The 1389 CE Battle of Kosovo ended the Serbian Empire and gave the Ottomans control over most of the land surrounding Constantinople. By 1402 CE, their conquests in the area were nearly complete, and the situation for the city of Constantinople looked bleak. Their situation was not entirely the result of poor luck and circumstance, however. Rather, they did much to ensure that they had little if any chance of stopping the advancing threat of the Ottomans.

There were two major civil wars fought in the Byzantine Empire during the 14th century. The first, lasting from 1321-1328 CE, was fought between Emperor Andronikos II and his grandson who desired the throne for himself. It was drawn out and not entirely conclusive, with his grandson ending up named co-Emperor as Andronikos III, but it was important for what it meant for the world surrounding the empire. It was during this time, in 1326 CE, that Orhan managed to capture Bursa, a city in Anatolia less than one hundred kilometers away from Constantinople itself, and made it his capital. Vast swaths of Anatolian territory was lost in this time due to the Byzantine Empire's distraction. When Andronikos III died in 1341 CE, it sparked another civil war which lasted until 1347 CE. This civil war permitted the Serbian Empire to seize significant territory in Macedonia and Epirus, again barely facing any challenge.

Both of these civil wars were, at their hearts, conflict between the increasingly powerful aristocrats and either the central government or the people at large. They both speak of an empire which was openly in decline and whose people had come to focus inward due to there being little point in looking outward. It is impossible to say for certain that the empire would have had any chance of halting the advance of their enemies, especially the Ottomans if they had not been so caught up in their own distraction. It is entirely possible that they were simply left too weak following the rise and fall of the Latin Empire to make a difference. What is certain, however, is that the Ottomans were greatly assisted by the disorganization and chaos found in their enemies when they began taking the Balkans by force.

In 1402 CE, with the Byzantine Empire left a mere shell of its former self, it was holding as its territory just the city of Constantinople itself and a small stretch of land to the west. Despite this, the Ottomans still struggled to take the city due to its continuing strategic advantage. The Bosporus Strait and the famous walls of the city were still formidable defenses, even if the city they sheltered was increasingly a dilapidated husk. The Byzantines were given unwitting aid in 1302 CE, however, when the Turko-Mongol leader Timur invaded Anatolia from the east. Timur was the founder of the Timurid Dynasty and desired more than anything to restore the old empire of Genghis Khan. A devout Muslim, Timur justified his invasions of powers such as the Ottomans as a necessary work to remove usurpers and restore proper Mongol rule. The Battle of Ankara in 1402 CE resulted in a crushing defeat for the Ottomans, and the capture of Sultan Bayezid I. What resulted from that was a civil war over which of the Sultan's sons would take power, and it raged until 1413 CE when Mehmed I took the throne.

The Ottoman civil war did result in the temporary loss of some territories such as Kosovo and Thessaloníki, but these losses did not last long. For Constantinople, their primary problem in the 14th century was a lack of manpower. Their city, which had at one point been the largest in Europe, had declined greatly under the weight of frequent attacks. Since 1261 CE, it had withstood assaults from the Latins, the Bulgarians, the Serbians, and the Turks, but with so little land to help sustain it, its population had suffered. In 1453 CE, when the final conquest occurred, the city managed to gather together a defensive force of seven thousand men, two thousand of which were from the west. Not helping this was the Black Plague, which had affected the city a century earlier, from 1343-1346 CE.

Efforts were made on the Byzantines' part to seek help from the west, but the Latin powers were reluctant to give it unless the people converted to the Latin Rite which they simply were not willing to do, even in the face of almost-certain defeat. That is not to say that no one in the west desired to help defend the city—thousands did volunteer—but the numbers paled in comparison to what was needed. When the siege began, the total population of the city stood at around fifty thousand people, with the invading Ottoman Army exceeding even that number. Though their situation was dire and aid seemed unlikely at best, it did not stop the final Byzantine Emperor, Constantine XI, from doing all that he could to shore up the defenses.

Constantine knew that the invasion was coming and did all that was possible to prevent the fall of the city. First, he had the walls first constructed on the order of Theodosius II repaired and reinforced; then he gathered all of the supplies and troops that he could for the defense. With so little land, money, and time, however, his best efforts ended up being paltry. In the end, he led a force of seven thousand troops against an army ten times its size. There was in all likelihood no amount of preparations capable of turning the tide on that battle.

The Ottoman forces were led by the ambitious young

Sultan Mehmed II, who would thereafter be known as Mehmed the Conqueror. He began his siege on April 6th of 1453 CE, and by May 29th the same year, it was finished, with Mehmed having accomplished what countless other would-be conquerors before him had failed to do: taking one of the most prized cities in the world. The first several assaults on the walls themselves ended as most others had before. Mehmed's losses were significant, and his advisors more than once became split on the subject of whether or not to continue the siege. On May 21st, he sent an envoy to Constantine XI, offering him and anyone else willing to do so the opportunity to flee with their goods and their lives intact. Constantine rebuked the offer, however, indicating that he intended to die in the defense of the city if that was what it came down to. On the 29th, after remobilizing his forces, Mehmed ordered the final assault. Throwing the bulk of his forces against the walls in waves, the onslaught turned out to be too much for the weary and depleted defenders to deal with.

Accounts differ on whether Constantine hanged himself during the final battle or removed his imperial regalia and charged with his men in one last futile stand, but regardless of which is true, by the end of the day, the final Byzantine Emperor was dead, and the city Constantine the Great had rededicated in 330 CE had fallen. It would thereafter become the capital of the rapidly expanding Ottoman Empire, remaining as such until its own fall in 1922 CE.

With that fall, there remained little left of the old Byzantine Empire. The independent states of Trebizond and Epirus, which came into being after the creation of the Latin Empire in 1204, continued on for a time, but by the end of the 15th century, they had also been conquered by the

Ottomans. If one considers the Byzantine Empire to have been the continuation of the Roman Empire all the way to the end, as many do, then the death of Constantine XI and the fall of Constantinople represented the final fall of Rome itself. An empire started in 27 BCE by Emperor Augustus lived on in one form or another until that day, and so it was that a nearly fifteen-thousand-year chapter of history came to a close.

Conclusion

Thank you for making it through to the end of *The Byzantine Empire: A Thousand Year History from Start to Finish*. Let's hope it was informative and helped you understand more about the history of one of the most fascinating empires in human history. The highs and lows of the incredibly inconsistent empire have intrigued people to this day. Just because you've finished the book, however, does not mean your move to learn more about the Byzantine Empire has to stop here.

If you want to learn more about the empire, its culture, its history, or anything else about it, there are plenty of further resources out there to help you. From documentary series to college lectures to other books, there are innumerable ways to seek out more and more information. It's difficult to fit a full millennium of history into any one book, and there are still plenty of materials out there to be learned. University professors who specialize in the subject have spent their whole lifetimes researching the empire and still keep finding new things about it.

Whether one wants to dedicate their lives to the study of this interesting period of history or just learn more for their own enjoyment and entertainment, the history of the Byzantine Empire contains no shortage of stories both epic and occasionally bizarre to amuse and inform people to this day.

Finally, if you found this book useful in any way, a review is always appreciated!

MAYA CIVILIZATION

A Complete Overview of The Maya History & Maya Mythology

© Copyright 2018 by Eric Brown

All rights reserved.

The following eBook is reproduced below with the goal of providing information that is as accurate and reliable as possible. Regardless, purchasing this eBook can be seen as consent to the fact that both the publisher and the author of this book are in no way experts on the topics discussed within and that any recommendations or suggestions that are made herein are for entertainment purposes only. Professionals should be consulted as needed prior to undertaking any of the action endorsed herein.

This declaration is deemed fair and valid by both the American Bar Association and the Committee of Publishers Association and is legally binding throughout the United States.

Furthermore, the transmission, duplication or reproduction of any of the following work including specific information will be considered an illegal act irrespective of if it is done electronically or in print. This extends to creating a secondary or tertiary copy of the work or a recorded copy and is only allowed with an expressed written consent from the Publisher. All additional rights reserved.

The information in the following pages is broadly considered to be truthful and accurate account of facts, and as such any inattention, use or misuse of the information in question by the reader will render any resulting actions solely under their purview. There are no scenarios in which the publisher or the original author of this work can be in any fashion deemed liable for any hardship or damages that may befall them after undertaking information described herein.

Additionally, the information in the following pages is

intended only for informational purposes and should thus be thought of as universal. As befitting its nature, it is presented without assurance regarding its prolonged validity or interim quality. Trademarks that are mentioned are done without written consent and can in no way be considered an endorsement from the trademark holder.

Table of Contents

Introduction 123

Chapter 1: The Maya People 125

Chapter 2: The Pre-Classic Period 2000 BCE–250 CE 129

Chapter 3: The Classic Period 250 BCE–900 CE................ 131

Chapter 4: The Post-Classic Period 950–1539 CE 134

Chapter 5: The Spanish Conquest 1511–1697 CE................137

Chapter 6: The Caste War of Yucatán 1847–1901 CE 141

Chapter 7: Maya Mathematics & Calendar.........................145

Chapter 8: Maya Religion 150

Chapter 9: Human Sacrifice 156

Chapter 10: Maya Architecture... 160

Chapter 11: Maya Culture 165

Chapter 12: Maya Technology 172

Chapter 13: Maya People Today 175

Conclusion..177

Introduction

Congratulations on downloading *Maya Civilization*, and thank you for doing so.

The following chapters will discuss what we famously refer to as the Maya Civilization—its history and the identity of its people. This civilization was believed to have sprouted around 1800 BCE during the Pre-Classic Period in what is now modern-day Belize. This book will cover their evolution from being a collection of small tribes into becoming an empire that sprawled across Mesoamerica and built flourishing city-states. In the Classic Period, the Maya reached their peak in terms of their artistic and mathematical development, their knowledge of astronomy, as well as the evolution of their calendar. They built huge pyramids that served as their temples, and those structures still stand today as historical sites.

Along with the history of their evolution, this book will also dive into the culture and religion of the Maya, with emphasis on their traditions, architecture, and technology. The Maya are especially famous for their tradition of human sacrifice, and this book will share information on that particular ritual, as well as on the reasons why the Maya became known for it. This book delves into many aspects of their culture to illustrate how they lived and grew as a civilization despite the frequent wars between the city-states. Lastly, this book also looks into the descendants of the Maya who are now mostly residing in Yucatán, Mexico and how they strive and fight to keep their traditions alive.

There are plenty of books on this subject on the market, so

thanks again for choosing this one! Every effort was made to ensure it is full of as much useful information as possible. Please enjoy!

Chapter 1:
The Maya People

The Maya were the indigenous people of Mexico and Central America, and they once inhabited lands composed of modern-day Mexico, as well as Guatemala, El Salvador, Honduras, and Belize to its south. This indicates that the Maya people had clustered in the central region of the South American continent, most likely to ensure they would be safe from the invasion of other Mesoamerican peoples.

Within that central region, the Maya are believed to have lived in three separate areas with unique characteristics: the northern Maya in the Yucatán Peninsula; the southern lands in northern Guatemala and in Mexico, Belize, and west Honduras; and in the mountainous terrain of southern Guatemala. The Maya of the lowland region is thought to have been the one to build the great stone cities we've come to associate with the entire civilization.

The term "Maya" for the civilization comes from the city of Mayapan, which was the last capital city of the Kingdom during the Post-Classic Period. These same regions today are still home to thousands of archaeological sites of the Maya Kingdom, many of which are still not fully explored. The most important cities include Chichen Itza, Coba, Copan Kalakmul, Tikal, and Uxmal. Surveys and excavations have been conducted by historians to learn more about this ancient people, and tourists are permitted to visit some of the sites.

People who trace their origin to the Maya refer to themselves by the terms Yucatec in the north and Quiche in the south.

These are descendants of the civilizations that lived on the same lands of Mesoamerica as their Maya ancestors. These descendants practice a somewhat modified version of the thousand-year-old rituals. They consider themselves linked to their ancestors through their similar languages and traditions and through their ethnic bonds. There are as many as 70 versions of the Maya language in the area, with most descendants also fluent in modern-day Spanish. Languages such as K'iche', Mam, and Q'anjob'al, which are common mainly in the regions of Guatemala, all have Mayan roots.

The Maya people were mostly farmers, with corn or *maize* being their staple crop. They also grew beans, squash, sweet potato, chili peppers, cocoa beans, vanilla beans, and tomatoes, as well as a variety of fruits. They used a farming technique called *milpa*, or what we call today as "slash-and-burn" farming. They would clear the land by cutting down all the trees and bushes and burning the foliage in the spring before the rainy season. Then they would plant their crops. This technique meant that the crop would only be fertile for a few years, so they also had to practice crop rotation every few seasons to ensure a healthy harvest. Besides farming, the Maya were also artisans, with extreme devotion to ceramics, painting, weaving, and textile work.

The Maya were said to have been "discovered" in the 1840s by English explorers John Lloyd Stephens and Frederick Catherwood. They were not the first explorers to visit the civilization of the Maya, but they were the first to document what they found through drawings, maps, and detailed stories. Stephens wrote his observations in *Incidents of Travel in Central America, Chiapas and Yucatán* (1841) and *Incidents of Travel in Yucatán* (1843), accompanied by Catherwood's illustrations.

Only a few Maya texts are believed to have survived the

Spanish conquest as the Spaniards had routinely destroyed Maya documents and artifacts. A famous text of the culture, written in the K'iche' language, provides an account of the mythology and history of the people. It begins with their creationism myth, which starts with the following: "This is the account of how all was in suspense, all calm, in silence; all motionless, quiet, and empty was the expanse of the sky."

The culture is said to have been known for its writers and storytellers, but the Maya have also accomplished mathematicians. They used a number system that even included the symbol for zero and allowed for longer calculations to be done more precisely. Their insight into astronomy was more advanced for its time than any other civilization as their astronomers constantly studied the movements of the sun, moon, and visible planets. They were very close in their calculations of the length of the solar year and the lunar cycle, only being off by 0.000198 and over by .0001, respectively.

Unfortunately, with the invasion of the Spaniards, alien diseases such as smallpox and typhoid infiltrated the native population and are thought to have reduced its number by as much as 90% around 1500 to 1600 CE. The spread of Catholicism and the Spanish language also overshadowed the Maya culture and forced its people to assimilate to a changing environment of colonization. The majority of their ancient documents were destroyed by the Spaniards, but a few bark books remain. Their history was also etched in stone, pottery, and cave drawings, giving modern archaeologists valuable insight into this civilization.

The causes for the Maya's fall are numerous, with archaeologists believing everything from political strife, economic instability, infighting between city-states, and environmental causes to be involved in their demise. One of the most central causes is that their cultivated land was not able to meet their food demands. Due to the slash-and-burn farming method, the land would only be viable for a few years at a time before they would be forced to move to another plot to grow their harvest. At its peak, there are believed to have been a population of almost 15 million people occupying the Maya cities. With an increase in population combined with the inability to provide food, it is only natural that economic and social unrest would occur, leading to battles between warring clans and city-states.

Chapter 2:
The Pre-Classic Period 2000 BCE–250 CE

The Maya are thought to have developed their first civilization in the Pre-Classic Period. Their unearthed settlements in what is now the region of Belize carbon-date to as far back as 2600 BCE. Scientists believe that the first villages were established around 1800 BCE in the Pacific coastline area of the Soconusco region. These people displayed classic early characteristics of the hunter-gatherers of the time as they occupied the rainforests and hills of that region.

The Maya eventually began making their livelihood as farmers. The evidence of corn in the area dates to before 2000 BCE, and surveys of the sediment show manipulation of the terrain. This could be from the burnings of the grass and the cultivation of the harvest. The cultural characteristics of the Maya people are thought to have emerged around 1800 BCE on the Guatemalan coast. The first signs of this were the temples built for various gods. Ceramics and household items have been excavated from ancient villages, and these dates as far back as 2000–1500 BCE. By 1000 BCE, the Maya had spread throughout southern Mexico, Belize, Honduras, and Guatemala.

It was during the Pre-Classic Period that the Maya are thought to have prospered in small villages and basic homes, their society sustained through agriculture. Maize, beans, squash, cacao, and other root crops were their major harvests, and the domestication of animals such as dogs and turkeys were also common. Most tribes depended heavily on their natural habitat and hunted or fished for meat. This sort of lifestyle of foraging for food and hunting as a tribe required a family-centered system to assist in one another's survival. It was also during this period that the culturally impacting Maya pottery and clay figurines began to emerge.

The cities of Palenque, Tikal, and Copan are believed to have been established in this era. The Maya had moved from the coast into the inland areas, though their communities had still been small. There was very little in terms of architectural advancement, only building homes and a temple at each settlement. By the Late Pre-Classic Period, a city known as El Mirador grew to almost 16 square kilometers. Cities began to trade with one another, and the exchange encouraged the propagation of crafts and the arts to influence the culture as a whole. Cities became more expansive, and a council of elders had usually been formed to ensure better management of a growing population in terms of city planning and harvesting decisions. Archaeologists believe that this is when the establishment of Maya kingship began, wherein the people install a ruler in a position of power and that ruler would be held responsible for all decisions made for the entire tribe. The presence of a royal dynasty would continue for the Maya until the Post-Classic Period.

In the coastal plains, Takalik Abaj and Chocoa grew to be two important cities. Meanwhile, Kaminaljuyu emerged in the highlands. What is now northern Belize appears to have been the primary location of the growing Maya Civilization in this era. During the Late Pre-Classic Period, the Maya were already beginning to build in their individual city-states. Tikal and other interior city centers were beginning public construction of plazas and markets, employing the local communities to assist one another with the projects. Archaeologists believe that major building projects involving Maya temples began in this period.

Chapter 3:
The Classic Period 250 BCE–900 CE

The Classic Period of the civilization is believed to have begun when carvings on stelae (statues of the leaders and rulers of the society) began to have dates from the Maya long-count calendar. Research shows the earliest date to have been 292 CE. This period marks the beginning of large construction projects, as well as a trend toward urbanism and artistic and intellectual progress. The Maya continued developing their arts and improving their fields of astronomy and mathematics. Multiple city-states emerged in the region to form alliances and enmities. The largest cities are thought to have populations from 50,000 to 120,000. The cities were connected by roads and a network of travel to ensure an open-trade route.

During the Early Classic Period, the city of Teotihuacán near Mexico City is believed to have intervened at Tikal and other cities to install a Teotihuacán-backed dynasty in 378 CE. The king of Tikal, Chak Tok Ich'aak I, is believed to have died the same day signaling a hostile takeover. The Teotihuacán army that led the invasion installed a new king, Yax Nuun Ahiin, and this resulted in a period where Tikal reigned over the most powerful city in the area by virtue of its alliance with Teotihuacán. This is evidenced by the pottery and architecture created in this era, which bore a resemblance to the Teotihuacán style.

The city of Tikal created an ally out of the city of Calakmul. This alliance was helpful, allowing lesser cities to join in the network and gain the benefit of protection and trade routes. It is common throughout the Classic Period that these cities would gain victory over a rival and then dip into a period of instability. Historians believe that as many as 80 Maya city-states may have existed side by side, in waves of peace and warfare. Tikal and Calakmul are believed to have engaged in warfare many times throughout the Classic Period, as rivalries between city-states often continued for generations after the rulers had died. Depending on the state of tensions between a certain city-state, the state could experience periods of economic growth or decline as well as see a dip in population after the loss of lives in battle.

In the south, Copán was the most influential city, founded in 426 CE by K'inich Yax K'uk' Mo'. This king had ties with Teotihuacán, and he used those ties to influence the city-state. Copán reached the height of development from 695 to 738 CE under the rule of Uaxaclajuun Ub'aah K'awiil. His reign ended when he was taken captive by a rival king of Quiriguá. He was taken to the victory city and decapitated in public. Historians believe the coup may have occurred at the urging of Calakmul to weaken the ally of Tikal. Alliances and rivalries like these between the rulers of city-states were common.

Like many cities from that area of Central America, the city of Teotihuacán is believed to have been abandoned around 900 CE, and the true cause remains unknown. During this period, cities in the northern region of the Yucatán Peninsula continued to be strong, thriving cities despite the mysterious fall of the southern ones. The region may have suffered a political collapse, ending current dynasties and causing unrest. Classic Maya cities used to be based solely on the authority of a single ruler who held all authority. This model was very rigid because it called for the ruler to make decisions regarding wars, harvests, and traditional rituals. Around this era, the individual rule was replaced by a council that did consist of individuals with noble lineage, but they also allowed priests, mathematicians, and other experts in their fields to provide counsel.

Archaeologists believe there was a swift and sudden migration from the south to the north due to the collapse of the powerful city-states. There could have also been environmental factors such as drought and soil degradation that were directly caused by overpopulation and increased food demands. Capital cities and other secondary cities are believed to have been abandoned within a period of 50 to 100 years. Cities stopped creating monuments that were once used to mark the passing of time. The last long-count date is believed to have been inscribed in 909 CE in the city of Toniná. Stelae were no longer raised, and the royal palaces of the rulers were abandoned. Mesoamerican trade routes of the era even shifted to bypass the previously bustling cities, indicating they were uninhabited by then.

Chapter 4:
The Post-Classic Period 950–1539 CE

Although major cities collapsed and the causes of the exodus are unclear, there did remain a Maya presence in regions that still had natural water resources. But unlike previous eras wherein abandoned lands were quickly resettled, this was not the case for this era. Instead, activity shifted to the north. The city of Chichen Itza dominated the earlier years of the Post-Classic Period from about 900 to 1250 CE, but after its decline in the 11th century, the region lacked a capital city until the city of Mayapan rose in the 12th century. This is the great city which is believed to have given the Maya its collective name. New cities formed near the capital and new trade networks began to connect neighboring regions. There are reasons to believe that new cities formed along the Gulf and the Caribbean coast to accommodate a trade network involving maritime goods.

The focus changed from a deeply religious nation in the Classic Period to a society focused on economic growth. Instead of relying on priests and the divine rule of kings, the Maya gave more praise to Chac, the Mayan rain god, to provide rain for their crops so they would flourish in their new home. Carvings of this god are found in the buildings of the Post-Classic Period cities such as Uxmal. This type of culture continued until the Spanish arrived in the 16th century.

The Maya Civilization came under the influence of the Toltecs, the name of the people who moved into Mexico after the fall of the city of Teotihuacán. There are significant evidence pointing to this, such as the Maya sculptures and architecture mirroring the Toltec style, as well as the Maya sacrifices to the Toltec rain god, Tlaloc, along with their rain god, Chac. Scholars have yet to pinpoint the political or economic relationship between the two olden cities, but it was clear the Toltecs did influence the Maya during this era.

There were many changes in the Post-Classic Period from the Classic Period. Kaminaljuyu, a city in what is now the region of Guatemala, was abandoned after nearly 2000 years of constant habitation. Cities moved farther inland into more mountainous regions with natural ravine and cavernous terrain. This could have been done so that they could use the natural terrain as protection if neighboring cities decided to wage an attack. With the lack of resources and people, the cities had no choice but to depend on the landscape for protection instead of on large armies, the way they used to.

The Maya of the Yucatán Peninsula had more challenges as they struggled to adjust to the dry climate of the area. They had to switch from using aboveground water sources and adjust to groundwater basins and sinkholes. Cenote Sagrado remains a sacred well in that area for having helped the Maya survive in their new settlement.

The major cities of the Post-Classic era include Chichen Itza and Mayapan. Other cities in the modern-day region of Belize include Santa Rita and Coba, as well Tayasal and Zacpeten in modern-day Guatemala. Mayapan, the capital city, is believed to have been abandoned due to political turbulence sometime in 1448 CE. The Maya states were often governed by a joint rule of a council of elders, but it seems that during this era, the council could appoint a supreme ruler and this may have caused division. This political turmoil along with environmental factors of drought and famine could have accounted for the abandonment of these cities along the Yucatán Peninsula even before the Spanish made contact in 1511.

The area of Guatemala was dominated by several reigning city-states, and the K'iche' had an empire in the Pacific coastal plain. In some regions without a flourishing capital city, the first Spanish explorers had reported thriving markets and lush coastal cities. Trade around the Yucatán cities was still occurring during the later years of the Post-Classic Period and even after the Spanish had arrived. The independent provinces that shared a common culture still managed to work together and maintained a network of good relations to ensure a surviving economy.

But with the ever-growing population and the continuing difficulty in meeting food demands, it is natural for archaeologists to believe that the Maya could not keep up with their provisional requirements. Recent studies have found evidence of environmental factors such as severe droughts, deforestation, and a decline in the population of game animals that would have all combined to create famine. Even the Maya remains dated to this era show severe signs of malnutrition. Though it is believed there was a brief renaissance and rebuilding before the Spanish arrived, it is assumed that the environmental condition did not improve, causing social anxiety and insecure living conditions among the city-states.

The Spanish began their conquest of the Maya in 1524 CE, but it would take them nearly 150 years to achieve complete victory. The main reason was that there was no central Mayan government, only individual city-states that needed to be subjugated separately. Another reason was that the Spanish arrived with dreams of finding gold, but the region did not possess vast quantities of precious metals, and the colonizers became disheartened many times throughout the fight.

Chapter 5:
The Spanish Conquest 1511–1697 CE

Before the year 1524 CE, which is commonly known as the fall of the Maya Empire, the Maya Civilization had had many encounters with explorers. The first recorded interaction between the Maya and the Europeans occurred on July 30, 1502, when Christopher Columbus arrived at Guanaja, Honduras. It was his fourth voyage to the Mesoamerican part of the world.

The account goes that Columbus had sent his brother Bartholomew to explore the nearby land. A large canoe approached, and Bartholomew Columbus boarded and found it to be a Maya trading vessel from Yucatán. The Europeans looted the rich cargo and seized the elderly captain to act as an interpreter for them. The rest of the canoe's passengers were allowed to leave. It is likely that this is where the first impressions and news of the strange pirates and bearded white male invaders spread along the area and came to be passed down. Such stories were even written in the Maya books of *Chilam Balam*.

It has also been told that in 1511, a Spanish vessel was shipwrecked along the Caribbean coast. Twelve survivors made it to the Yucatán coast. They were captured by the Maya and killed in rituals of human sacrifice, but two managed to escape and tell the tale of what they lived through. During the time period of 1517 and 1519, three other Spanish crews visited the coastline of Yucatán and battled with the Maya.

The notion that the Maya were driven from their cities by

Spanish conquistadors is not entirely correct. Most major cities were already abandoned when the Spaniards first arrived. Though the K'iche' and the Cachiquel groups in Guatemala were attempting to rebuild, they were foiled when they came under the control of the Aztecs. Additionally, conflicts within the Maya lands had already resulted in divisions between the city-states, causing the empire to fall from its former glory.

The Spanish colonization of the Maya lands officially began in 1521 when Francisco de Montejo petitioned the King of Spain for the right to conquer the Yucatán. In 1524, Hernán Cortés conquered the Aztec Empire and sent his lieutenant, Pedro de Alvarado, to investigate and conquer the nearby Maya city-states in what is now northern Guatemala. It is believed he defeated Tenochtitlan on October 12, 1524, with 300 infantry, 4 cannons, 180 cavalry units, and up to 3000 warriors from Mexico. Before that, he had marched through the Maya province of Acalan where he recruited up to 600 more soldiers. He had a difficult journey southward along the Maya Mountains and lost most of his horses due to the terrain. The group got lost near Lake Izabal and came close to starvation before they captured a Maya who led them to safety. Having found them already weak, Alvarado easily conquered the nearby city-states after preying on the rivalries between the rulers to cause infighting. The introduction of new European diseases also decimated the struggling population, which had no immunity to these foreign illnesses.

The K'iche' capital, Q'umarkaj, fell to Alvarado in 1524. Next came the collapse of Zaculeu and the Itza capital of Nojpeten. During the Battle of Utatlan, the K'iche' Maya was defeated. Unlike the Aztec which had been a centralized community, the Maya had been spread out into city-states, and they resisted Spanish rule with bloody rebellions for nearly a hundred years. Unlike their victories over the Mesoamerican empires in Mexico and Central America, defeating the Maya had not been a swift undertaking, but eventually, the Spaniards won against the last Mayan city in the Peten in 1697.

The Conquistadors had traveled to the Mesoamerican region in hopes of finding gold and silver. Trace amounts were found along Columbia and Ecuador and were transported back to Spain, but these regions were not as rich in metals as the Spanish had been led to believe. They enslaved the Maya and divided up the land between the generals of the army and the government bureaucrats who came from Spain to assist in ruling the new nations.

The Maya were required to convert to Christianity, and those who refused had been arrested and tortured. The Spanish were also active in destroying Mayan artifacts. Much of their culture, writing, and art were destroyed; only a few sacred texts had been saved and passed down to the succeeding generations. Many of the native peoples suffered. Bloody rebellions were common as the Maya were reluctant subjects of this new foreign government. They were repressed forcibly, and loss of life was significant. A man by the name of Bartolomé de Las Casas passionately argued for the rights of the Maya in the Spanish court; his efforts were ultimately thwarted, but they were not without any positive impact.

Some remote Maya villages did survive on their own and continued their day-to-day life. They maintained a traditional diet of tortilla, maize, and beans and kept their traditional crafts of basket-weaving and ceramic-making. It is assumed that their agriculture became easier and more advanced with the help of the steel tools that the Spaniards brought, and trade and education in the local crafts continued well after the conquest. The administration of the colonies would also encourage the traditional economy; there was a demand for local goods. However, the Mayan ceramics and textiles would thereafter take on a more European leaning.

Chapter 6: The Caste War of Yucatán 1847–1901 CE

A 19th century revolt by the indigenous Maya people of Yucatán, Mexico that lasted for nearly fifty years is known today as the Caste War of Yucatán. The Maya revolted against the European descendants called the Yucatecos, who held the most political and economic control in the region. The inhabitants of the northwest Yucatán region fought with the independent Maya people of the southeast.

During the Spanish colonial times, there existed a caste system wherein those born in Spain with pure Spanish blood stands at the top and the indigenous people of the land lies at the very bottom. The indigenous population was concentrated in the Campeche-Mérida region. In the Yucatán region, the Maya outnumbered the European-descended groups by nearly 3:1, and it was by 5:1 near the east in terms of the population ratio. The elites controlled the Maya, and the Church and the military aligned with the stronger classes.

The success of the Mexican War of Independence inspired the subjugated Maya people in the Yucatán. They organized their own resistance to gain independence from Spain, and they joined with the Mexican government which aimed for centralization of the city-states despite many provinces revolting against the notion. After the war against Texas, the Mexican government imposed a number of high taxes to bear the costs, even imposing a trade tax.

On May 2, 1839, a protest led by Santiago Imán created a rival government in Tizimín. He and his followers took over

Valladolid, Izamal, Espita, and lastly, the city of Mérida on the Yucatán Peninsula. He convinced the Maya population to join the cause and even gave them access to weapons for the first time since the Spanish Conquest. With the support of the Maya, he prevailed in battle and proclaimed Yucatán to be an independent republic as of 1841.

The head of the Mexican government, Antonio López de Santa Anna, refused to accept their independence and imposed a blockade. Invasion followed, and the Yucatán struggled against the authority of the Mexicans and its divided factions. One faction based in Campeche led by Santiago Méndez feared reintegration and a sudden attack on the region by the United States at the northern border. In Mérida, Miguel Barbachano leaned toward reintegration to gain the safety of Mexico. Both leaders convinced many Maya citizens into their armies as soldiers.

The War started in defense of Indian land against private ownership due to the increased production of the agave plant. This was an industrial fiber at the time, harvested to make rope. Once the plant's value was discovered, the wealthy Spanish Yucatecos created huge plantations to cultivate it on a large scale and began to encroach on Maya communal lands. They abused Maya workers and treated them poorly, underpaying them for their hard labor.

Santiago Méndez, who was leading a faction near Campeche, arrested Antonio Ay, the principal Maya leader of Chichimilá, and executed him in the Valladolid town square. Méndez burned down the entire town of Tepich, and several other Maya towns were destroyed, with many people killed in the subsequent months. Cecilio Chi, Maya leader of Tepich, attacked the city of Tepich on July 30, 1847, and decreed that any non-Maya would be killed. By 1848, the Maya forces had taken over the majority of Yucatán except for the walled cities of Campeche and Mérida along the southern coast. In an 1849 letter, Chi wrote that Méndez's goal was to "put every Indian, big and little, to death" but that the Maya had responded in kind. He wrote, "It has pleased God and good fortune that a much greater portion of them [whites] than of the Indians [have died]."

Miguel Barbachano, the Yucatecan governor, prepared to evacuate the city of Mérida but could not send out the order due to a lack of paper in the capital city. Troops managed to invade the city and make significant advances.

The reason for the Maya's defeat is unclear. Historians believe they might have abandoned their posts to tend their fields, or they may not have been able to feed their army any longer and became frustrated with the long war efforts.

By 1850, the Maya occupied two regions and a stalemate had developed among the northwestern tribes. Positioned in the middle was the jungle region. In 1850, an apparition of the "Talking Cross" appeared to inspire the Maya to keep fighting. The apparition was believed to have been God communicating with the Maya. Chan Santa Cruz, translated to mean "Small Holy Cross," became a religious mecca for the resistance and inspired new religious meaning in the soldiers and supporters. The followers of the Cross became known as the "Cruzob" people.

The largest independent Maya state was called Chan Santa Cruz, and its capital city was given the same name. The United Kingdom recognized Chan Santa Cruz as an independent "de facto" nation due to the trade routes between the region and British Honduras. This resulted in a signed international treaty, though it was never formally ratified by either party. The region had extensive trade relations with British Honduras and had a significantly larger militia than the British colony. For these reasons, the British felt it advantageous to maintain good relations.

When the Maya laid siege on the city of Bacalar and killed British citizens, the British Government assigned Sir Spenser St. John to break relations with the indigenous free states, particularly the Maya free state. In 1893, the British Government signed the Spenser Mariscal Treaty that ceded the Maya state's lands to Mexico. Chan Santa Cruz was then occupied by the Mexican army.

The conflict ended in 1915 when the region agreed to recognize the Mexican government. General Francisco May signed a formal treaty with the government of Mexico to represent another step taken toward peace. In September 1915, the Mexican government sent General Salvador Alvarado to restore order in Yucatán. He worked to implement reforms which eliminated conflicts between the regions.

The last skirmish in the area is documented as having occurred in April 1933 when the Mexican army took a force into a remote village that never recognized the establishment of Mexican law. Two Mexican soldiers along with five Maya citizens were killed in the village of Dzula. This is the last historically noted incident that occurred in a conflict that lasted almost 90 years.

Chapter 7: Maya Mathematics & Calendar

At its cultural peak around 250 to 900 CE, the Maya created a very sophisticated numbering system that was possibly the most advanced in the entire world during the time. The Maya, like many Mesoamerican cultures of the period, used a vigesimal numbering system that was founded on a base of 20 units: 0–19 with zero included as a numeral. This was most likely inspired by the natural use of the fingers and toes to count. The numerals had three symbols: zero represented by a shell shape, five by a bar, and one by a single dot. Adding and subtracting became simpler when they only needed to count dots and bars, and this allowed even the uneducated to do calculations related to trade and commerce easily.

Because of the simplicity of these symbols, it is believed that the Maya used objects from nature itself when practicing their math—i.e., real sticks, stones, and shells had been used to manipulate numbers and work on problems. Scientists have found that all the major mathematical functions (addition, subtraction, division square roots, multiplication) could be performed using this simple base system. The Maya mathematical system is even now being taught in Yucatán, Mexico, where the descendants of the Maya people are most greatly concentrated. It is especially taught to the indigenous children in the area to encourage understanding and appreciation of their culture.

Maya numbers are written from bottom to top instead of horizontally like most of the world does today. For example, the number 12 is presented as two bars and two dots on top.

The number 19 is three bars and four dots on top. Numbers greater than 19 were represented the same way, but with a dot placed above the number for each group of 20 it had. This place value format used the powers of 20: 1, 20, 400, 8000, and 160,000. The number 32 would contain all the symbols for the number 12, but with an additional dot to signify the addition of 20. The number 401 would use a dot in the first position, a zero in the second and another dot in the third to first signify 400 (20 × 20) and then the addition of one. It is commonly believed that the society used cocoa beans on the ground to do their calculations.

The names for common numerals are as follows:

0: xix im

1: hun

2: caa

3: ox

4: can

5: hoo

6: uac

7: uuc

8: uaxac

9: bolon

10: lahun

20: hun kal

40: ca kal

60: ox kal

80: can kal

100: hoo kal

200: ka hoo kal

300: ox hoo kal

400: hun bak

800: ca bak

1200: ox bak

1600: can bak

2000: hoo bak

8000: pic

160,000: calab

3,200,000: kinchil

64,000,000: alau

It is believed that the Pre-Classic Maya and their Mesoamerican neighbors formulated the concept of the zero integers around 30 BCE. There is archaeological evidence that shows them working with integers up to the hundreds of millions. It would sometimes take lines of dashes and circles to represent the number. The concept of a zero was unknown in most Classic societies with the exception of the Gupta Empire in India, but zero days and zero years exist in the Maya calendar, and the Maya society understands its value and how it may be used to multiply and add enormous numbers.

The Maya also considered some numbers sacred over other numbers. The number 20, which formed the basis of their counting system, was one of those numbers, most likely because of the ten toes and ten fingers that a human could count on. The number five also had religious significance as this was the number of digits on a foot or a hand. Thirteen was considered to be a number for the original Maya gods. The number 52 was sacred and was established to be the number of years in a "bundle," which is a unit that the Maya used as a concept similar to the concept of "century" we use today. The number 400 was considered to represent the Maya gods of the night.

The Maya also used head glyphs as numerical symbols to represent the gods. The number one was depicted as a young earth goddess, the number two for a god of sacrifice, and so on. The glyphs are very similar to each other, and this presented archaeologists with some difficulty when decoding them. The number was also sometimes written as compounds. The number 13 would use the glyph for 10 plus the glyph for number three. This combined with the usual shells, bars, and dots that formed the base level of Maya mathematics.

Mathematicians were an important and respected part of Maya society. This is evident in the Maya wall paintings discovered by historians long after the society collapsed. Maya mathematicians and their scribes can be identified as the ones carrying number scrolls in their arms. Most historians agree that the first mathematician identified on a glyph in wall art was a female figure, indicating that the Maya did not prefer male mathematicians over female.

Due to this very precise concept of math, the Maya were more accurate than other societies in their astronomical observations and calculations. Considering that they were working from only naked eye observation, their numbers are very comparable to modern data. They charted the movements of Jupiter, Venus, the moon, Mars, and Mercury. They also tracked the position of the sun along the horizon to gauge when the seasons would change. They were especially captivated by the constellations in the night sky and believed them to be the gods watching over them. The estimated the length of a lunar month to be 29.5308 days. Today's modern value is 29.53059. They calculated the length of a solar year to be 365.242 days, extremely close to today's modern value of 365.242198 and far more accurate than any used in Europe at the time. The length of 365 days means that the calendar only fell out of step with the seasons by one day every four years. Again, this was achieved while working only with naked eye observation. By comparison, the Julian calendar used in Europe during the Roman Empire had an error of one day every 128 years.

It is believed the Maya had two calendars: the Tzolkin and the Haab. The Tzolkin had 260 days which was divided into 13 "months" of 20 days each. These months were named after gods while the 20 days were numbered by using the digits 0 to 19. This was their religious ritual calendar. Every

52 years counted as an interval, and after that time period, the calendar would reset itself and begin from zero. The Haab calendar was a 365 day civil calendar which consisted 18 months and contained dates of religious and agricultural events that the entire society would participate in. The Maya had a great understanding of celestial bodies for the time period and could even predict solar eclipses. They used the astrological cycles to aid in harvesting and planting their crops, and these events would also be labeled on the Haab calendar.

It is important to note that despite the advanced thinking of their time, the Maya and Mesoamerican mathematical numbering systems had no influence on the European and Asian systems due to a significant geographical divide. This works reciprocally—they were also not influenced by the European and Asian systems, and all advancements in their thinking are credited solely to the Maya society. Their mathematics allowed the Maya to have one of the most accurate calendar measurements of all the ancient societies, to construct huge step-pyramids, and to engage in a complex system of trade with neighboring societies.

Chapter 8: Maya Religion

The Maya religion is based on the belief that everything in the world contains *k'uh* (sadness), and this is used to explain the spirituality of all animate and inanimate objects in the universe. The belief is that this establishes sanctity between all life forms—between the earth and humans.

When beginning to look at the Maya creation myth, it is critical to differentiate between the two sources that have been unearthed. These include the books *Popol Vuh* and *Chilam Balam. Popol Vuh* is connected to the traditional Maya highland region in what is now the country of Guatemala. It contains the traditional myths, histories, and prophecies that historians associate with the Maya. The anthologies of *Chilam Balam* are associated typically with the Yucatán area of Mexico and were written by a priest whose name translated to *Chilam Balam*. These books are from around 1500 CE after Spanish Conquistadors had already invaded the Maya empire, and historians believe there is Spanish influence on this in the stories of *Chilam Balam.*

Earth is believed to have created by Huracán, the sky and wind god. The earth and sky were connected, and there was no space in between for anything living to flourish. A Ceiba tree was planted. The tree's roots grew into the underworld, and the branches grew up in the atmosphere. The trunk grew big enough to leave room on earth for animals, humans, and plants to roam across the land. Animals and plants were believed to be in existence long before humans, but the Maya believed the gods were unhappy with them because animals could not speak to praise the gods. Because of this sole reason, the gods created humans to praise them.

There are three creation stories detailed in the *Popol Vuh* of the highland Maya: people made from mud, people made from wood, and people made from maize. The first creation tale told that people were made from mud, but they were not the most productive and were not very rational or capable of high-thinking. According to ancient texts, the men and women "spoke but had no mind." They were not even technically mortal. The gods were displeased with them and destroyed them with water.

Next, the gods created women from reeds and men from wood. These creations could pass as human beings, but they possessed no souls and they did not properly honor the gods. They were also immortal and supposedly died for only three days before rising from the dead. (This very closely follows the stories of Christianity.) This society was destroyed by being boiled in hot water. The Maya believed that those who survived their destruction became the monkeys that roamed their jungles.

The third creation was that of the modern-day Maya humans. The Maya believe they are created from maize dough and possessed the blood of the gods. The first batch created consisted of four men and four men. They were believed to be too wise by the gods and were destroyed by them as well, fearing that they'll become threats. But the Heart of the Heaven, or Huracán the sky god, clouded their eyes and minds so they would become less wise and less of a threat to their superiors. In this story, Huracán is known as the Heart of Earth, Heart of Heaven, and Heart of Sky for his mercy to this creation.

Despite the different creation myths, the most important note historians made was the notion of destruction common among these societies. New humans were created then destroyed to make room for another civilization. This is not synonymous with the Maya notion of "the end of the world" but simply recognizes that they believe in the notion of the end of humanity and in a new civilization created by the mercy of their gods. The gods destroyed these civilizations because they would not worship them, and they would not have unworthy subjects who could not praise them.

Though there are Maya deities, the most significant gods often morphed with the less notable ones and shared characteristics of both gods at the same time. Some could even have conflicting traits. These diverse and fluid personalities that shift many times make it difficult for historians to identify and isolate each Maya deities. This is true for their appearance as well.

Huracán is a significant god as shown in the creation myth. He is also known as the "giver of life" in prayer in the *Popol Vuh* book. This prayer suggests he was important as a creator. He is associated with the Quiche Maya of Guatemala and supposedly created the earth and took mercy on the maize people who are the current human civilization. He is the lord of the fire, storms, and wind.

Itzam Ná and Ix Chebel Yax are two gods associated with creation as well. Itzam Ná is drawn as a long-nosed old man, or sometimes as an iguana. His wife is Ix Chebel Yax who is very high in the hierarchy of the gods. K'inich Ajaw is sometimes known as God G or Kinich Ahau, the "Sun-faced Lord." He is portrayed as being born in the East and aging and setting in the West just as the sun does. He was a war advisor to the underworld and could also transform into a jaguar. Sun deities are to be feared and worshipped at the same time; though they give the life-giving properties of the sun, they can also send too many rays to create drought and ruin the harvest. Chac was the counterpart god to K'inich Ajaw, known as God B. He is believed to be both human and reptile and is often depicted with a serpent, lightning bolt, or an axe. This god is sometimes depicted as being blue with whiskers. The Maya believed he also had the power to create thunder, lightning, and clouds. He was also to be feared and worshipped because he brought rains for the people and crops but also created floods. He demanded blood sacrifices for payment for the rains.

The maize god, Hun H'unahpu, was also considered an important celestial being and was referred to as God E. He was believed to have created the modern humans that lived in the lowland Yucatec Maya using his own maize and blood. He was seen as a symbol of fertility and was depicted as a handsome young man with long black hair.

God K, or K'awil, is the god responsible for protecting the royal bloodline and was also linked to lightning. He is depicted with piercings of a torch and carrying a blade and has a snout on one foot and a snake on the other. He is believed to have discovered maize and cocoa when he struck his lightning bolt on a mountain.

Ix Chel, or God O, is the goddess of the rainbows. Rainbows symbolize harmony and peace in Western culture, but this is not the case for the Maya. They believed that rainbows were the "flatulence of demons" and that they brought sickness. When her form was believed to bring bad luck, she was drawn as clawed and fanged for this reason. But due to the often duplicitous traits of the gods the Maya attached to their deities, Ix Chel could also represent childbirth and fertility. When pictured in those contexts, she is depicted as very beautiful and youthful.

A popular legend in Maya religious culture is that of the Hero

Twins, two brothers named Xbalanque and Hunahpu who survived adventures in the underworld. Their stories are chronicled in the *Popol Vuh*. The Twins' father was the god Hun H'unahpu—he and his brother were lured to the underworld to be decapitated. But because he was immortal, his head survived and gave fruit. His head then fell onto the goddess Xquic who gave birth to the Hero Twins.

These twins faced many challenges in their heroic story to return home, but the most significant was their journey through Xibalba, the Maya underworld. They were summoned there after they played a noisy ballgame that disturbed the underworld lords. The lords challenged the twins, but the brothers were cunning and wise, getting the best of the lords. Hunahpu and Xbalanque grew bored with the challenges and thought of a way to escape by disguising themselves. They performed a trick for the lords wherein they sacrificed a person and brought the person back to life. The lords were impressed and asked them to perform the trick on them. But Xbalanque and Hunahpu were smart and seized the opportunity. Instead of bringing the lords back to life, the twins left them dead and declared the underworld as a place for sinners to be held captive. The Hero Twins and the lords of Xibalba are believed to be night stars. The Maya believe that their kings would have to follow the trials of Xbalanque and Hunahpu in the underworld after their death in order to make it to heaven.

Regarding hell and heaven, the Maya believed in various levels and called them the underworld, middle, and upper world. The upper world consists of thirteen levels while the middle world was only one level. The underworld contained nine different levels of hell. The Ceiba tree is believed to grow through all the levels and provided the five cardinal directions they believed in—the four directions and the center. The most important direction to the Maya was the east where the sun rises. They associated it with rebirth because they believed the sun is born daily.

Chapter 9:
Human Sacrifice

Despite the common tales of Maya human sacrifice, not all religious rituals required it. Sacrifices were most commonly performed in a mix of religious ceremonies because blood was seen as the nourishment for the deities. Sacrifices were also given during important ceremonies such as dedicating a new building or celebrating the enthronement of a new ruler. Human sacrifice is evident in Maya culture from at least the Classic Period (250–900 CE) right until the final stages of the Spanish conquest. These events are written in the Maya hieroglyphic texts of the era and are also depicted in Maya art. Even archaeological analysis of skeletal remains shows evidence of human sacrifice.

Several methods were used by the Maya to perform their rituals of human sacrifice, including decapitation, heart removal, and arrow sacrifice. The method depended on which type of ceremony was occurring. The sacrifice of an enemy king was considered the most important ritual. It required some sort of playacting, a reenactment of the capture of the ruler in front of a crowd—the decapitation of the Maya maize god by the death gods.

In 738 CE, the king K'ak' Tiliw Chan Yopaat of Quiriguá captured his overlord, Uaxaclajuun Ub'aah K'awiil and then decapitated him. Historians believe that these events are illustrated in the Maya texts by the symbol of an axe. Sacrifice by decapitation is also depicted in Maya art. They may have taken place after the victim was beaten, burnt, or disemboweled. Decapitation sacrifices are also shown on ancient reliefs at Chichen Itza in two of the ballcourts.

Ballcourt sacrifices were common to reenact the story where the Hero Twins decapitated their ballgame opponents.

In the Post-Classic Period, the common form of sacrifice was heart extraction. This was influenced by their neighbors, the Aztec Empire. These most commonly occurred at the steps of the pyramid or in the temple's courtyard. The sacrificial victim was stripped naked, painted blue, and forced to wear an elaborate headdress. Four attendants, also painted blue and representing the four cardinal directions, stretched the sacrifice out over a large stone. This would push the victim's chest out. An official called the *nacom* used a knife to saw into the ribs and cut out the beating heart. The knife was most commonly made of flint stone. The *nacom* would pass the heart to the priest, or *chilan*, who smeared the blood upon the temple to complete the sacrifice.

For some rituals, the helpers may have even thrown the victim down the stone steps where they would be skinned, except sometimes their heads and feet would be kept. The *chilan* would dress in the victim's skin and perform a dance to symbolize the rebirth of life. If it was not a courageous warrior who became a sacrificial victim, then the corpse could even be cut into pieces and eaten by other attendants and bystanders. If it was a warrior, the hands and feet would be given to the *chilan* who, if they were also a soldier, kept the bones as a trophy.

Arrow sacrifice involved being killed with bows and arrows. This type of sacrifice is recorded as early as the Classic Period on the walls of the Tikal Temple in graffiti art. The victim was stripped of clothing and painted blue. They would be tied to a stake while a ritualistic dance was performed around them. Genital blood would be drawn and smeared along the temple. The victim's heart would be marked with a white mark to present it clearly as a target to the archers during the arrow ceremony. The dancers performed their traditional dance in front of the victim and would shoot arrows until the chest was filled with them.

The most common sacrifice was bloodletting, which is the spilling of blood in human sacrifice. The Maya practice of bloodletting was mostly done by the royal line. The Maya believed the gods had spilled their blood to create humanity, so they now demanded human blood in return. Along with human blood, the Maya would also offer to the god's other precious items such as masks, human bone, shells, gold, and ceremonial tools.

Bloodletting was common during significant dates on the Maya calendar such as births, new kings rising to the throne, and anniversaries. Royals who participated in the practice spent many days before the ritual preparing themselves through purification. Both women and men from the royal family were to perform these rituals, and they made sacred tools to use on themselves. The tools were most commonly made of stingray spines and had glyphs carved into them to show religious significance. Blood was let from various parts of the body, and it was often a contest to see which area could provide the most significant amount of blood. Another form of overlooked communication with the gods was lowering children into wells in the belief that they could speak to the gods. After hours in the well, the children would be pulled back up so they could relay the message of the gods.

It is important to note that there were many skirmishes with the Spanish regarding human sacrifice. The Spanish ship, Santa María de la Barca, set sail along the coast of Central America in 1511. After thirteen days, half the survivors made it to the Yucatán coast where they were seized by a Mayan lord, Halach Uinik. The captain of the ship and four companions were sacrificed, and their flesh was served at a feast. In 1529, another disastrous Spanish assault on Uspantán occurred and the captives were sacrificed to one of the Hero Twins. Such occurrences were common until the 16th century, in which many shipwrecked survivors and Spanish missionaries were sacrificed. This served only to exacerbate the relations between the Spanish and the Maya.

It is important to note that the Maya religion held no concept whatsoever that there was anything wrong with human sacrifice. It was not done out of spite or revenge to the individual. In fact, they simply believed the individuals being sacrificed were moving on and that their sacrifice would greatly please the gods, giving them a higher rank in heaven.

Chapter 10: Maya Architecture

Thanks to their advanced mathematical skill for that time period, the Mayan architects built cities of stone that remain to this day, long after the decline of their civilization. These stone structures were set with hydraulic cement and enabled the Maya structure to survive centuries of abandonment, followed by excavation from scientists to learn about these ancient civilizations. Some remain standing to this day and serve as tourist sites. The Maya decorated these buildings with detailed stone carvings and paint, often depicting the important political or religious occurrences of their city-state as a way of recording their history.

The Maya designed their city-states using what architects call today as a plaza-central plan. They arranged clusters of important buildings around a central open plaza layout. This placed important buildings such as the palaces, temples, and schools in the location of residential areas. Historians have found these were not arranged as orderly as it sounds. Due to the Maya building their city-states on uneven terrain to avoid floods and for their city's protection, these plaza shapes could be very irregular. In the center of the cities, the temples, palaces, and a ball court to play the game of Poc-a-Toc were linked to dense residential areas that grew into sparser villages the further away they are from the city. Stone walkways linked the residential areas.

The Maya kings lived in stone palaces near the city temples, but the commoners lived in small houses away from the center. The homes tended to be bunched close together for anthropological needs. Having extended family living close by provided support when necessary, especially for couples with young children. The houses were made mostly of wood, poles, and thatch. As the wood and leaves of the walls wore away due to natural weathering, they would take it as a sign to rebuild on the same foundation. Because the commoners' ground was further away from the high ground of the city center, most of these homes have been lost due to flooding or the encroaching jungle terrain.

Maya temples were built of limestone with platforms on the top where wooden structures could be erected. They were built with astronomy and the alignment of the sun, moon, or other visible planets in mind. For example, the Lost World Complex at Tikal has a temple pyramid that faces three other temples. When standing at one pyramid you can see the other temples aligned with the rising and setting sun. Temples were built in the shape of pyramids with steep steps built to the top. These provided a platform where religious ceremonies and sacrifices took place and a point where all citizens could gather in the courtyard and watch.

Archaeologists have been able to decipher Maya historical events and the detail behind their religious ceremonies due to the artwork and glyphs carved into the stones of the temple. The famous Hieroglyphic Stairway at a temple in Copán is an example of detailed stone carvings that remain to this day. Because there are so few remaining artifacts from the Maya era, these carvings give an important insight for historians to piece together the history of the Maya. The pyramids also acted as tombs for the Maya rulers and their families, sacrifice victims, as well as precious goods that were needed to be kept with the royal family. Because of the necessity for more space, archaeologists have found that the outside pyramid structures sometimes reveal complete but diminishing pyramids inside

A notable example of a typical Maya temple structure would be the Palenque's Temple of Inscriptions believed to be built around 700 CE. A single staircase climbs several levels to the top to a platform that has several chambers, believed to be for the priests. The pyramid has nine levels that are said to represent the nine levels of the Maya underworld, Xibalba. There is a secret passageway that descends to the tomb of King Pakal in the center. The passageway has thirteen steps to represent the thirteen Maya heavens.

Another unique example of Maya architecture is the Pyramid of the Magician at Uxmal which is believed to have been built around 600 CE. It is distinctive because of the rounded corners that make it seem almost oval in shape. It is the only one of its kind that has been found in the standing structures left by the Maya Civilization.

The royal palaces were built from the same materials as the other homes and in the same manner—limestone with rubber, wooden structures on top, and a thatch roof. Some roofs would have corbelled roofing where flat stones would be piled upon one another in overlapping patterns for protection. This type of roofing is found more commonly in structures dating the Post-Classic Period, indicating that the Maya must have found this more successful and implemented it in later structures over the earlier thatch roof.

The palaces were built as spacious, open buildings with courtyards and other smaller structures that acted as homes to servants, outdoor eating areas, or watch towers for guards. There were plenty of rooms to act as cooking areas, sleeping quarters, classrooms for children, and luxury rooms that double as steam rooms and bathrooms. Some palaces were significantly larger than others, leading historians to believe they also acted as offices where councilmen met to discuss wars, trade, and agriculture. These palaces were the place where royalty and noblemen met with commoners and hosted visiting royalty from other city-states. Statewide feasts, ceremonies for the new king, royal dances, and community events took place at the palaces as well.

Historians believe religious ceremonies were also hosted at the royal palaces and not just at the pyramids, based on the evidence of the Nunnery complex at Uxmal. The northern building of that palace has thirteen doorways representing the thirteen levels of heaven that the Maya believe in. The southern building has nine doorways to represent the nine levels of the underworld, and the western building has seven doorways which were considered the mystic number of the earth.

The ceremonial game of Poc-a-Toc was a pastime for the common and nobility alike, but the game also held important religious and spiritual significance, with the losers, or sometimes even the winners, being sacrificed in the belief they would make it to heaven. The game's ball courts were huge rectangular fields with sloped walls. In the later Post-Classic Period, the walls were changed to vertical walls. They were placed distinctly near the center of the city for their importance to the culture. Some cities even had more than one. The most famous one from the Maya is the court found at Copán believed to be built around 800 CE. It is perfectly framed in the view of the hills around the area. Archaeologists believe that since these courts had a religious significance, they were positioned carefully between the north and the south to maintain the balance of the earthly world and the underworld.

Small stone structures that acted as sweat baths were also found, with huge stones where heated water was poured. There were often small adjoining spaces to be used for changing clothes. They are usually found by ball courts and in the royal palace area and were used for both cleaning and religious purposes.

Another unique aspect of Maya architecture is the corbelled arches they built to resemble the classic arch that originated from the ancient Greek. The stones would be aligned in long patterns to make the appearance of an arch in an inverted "V" shape. The blocks were stacked in successive steps from opposite sides and closing in at the center. The arches had severe limitations due to it being structurally unstable. For the arch to be durable, it would have to be tall and narrow and often made the rooms dark and narrow due to a lack of light. These arches became known as the Maya arches and formed the base for all Maya structures.

Chapter 11:
Maya Culture

Marriage was an important religious ritual and an event of celebration in Maya culture. Marriages were arranged and the parties come from the same social class. Couples could be matched at a very young age, sometimes even promised to each other as infants. Historians believe that the ages of Maya individuals at the time of marriage were linked to the Maya population as a whole: when the population was low, marriages would occur even if the individuals were young so they could reproduce sooner and repopulate.

Priests preformed the marriage ceremonies most often at the bride's home. They would burn incense to pray for a fruitful marriage. A feast would be cooked to celebrate the joining. The exchanging of gifts were common, either gold or precious items of significance. If the marriage was considered not successful by either party, the couple could divorce. Although there is no ritual for a divorce described in Maya text, historians have found that it was an acceptable option, and the couple could peacefully part ways.

The typical Maya family averaged five to seven members according to modern archaeologists. The family all lived together and followed traditional gender roles: the men farmed and hunted while the women would cook and weave in the home. The girl children helped their mothers while the boys, when old enough, would learn from their fathers and help with physical labor. Children only went to school if they came from a noble family. The role of the extended family was common among the Maya. Often, newlywed couples would live with the groom's parents until they had a child of their own. Then they might leave to establish their own home. Later in life, elderly parents might return to their children's home to be taken care of in their old age.

A typical home for a Maya family would depend on their region. Groups who lived in south Guatemala would live in one-room huts built out of poles and covered with dried mud for protection from the elements. Other groups in the highlands would live in houses with tile roofs, the walls made of boards or poles. Most of the Maya were farmers, so the diet of corn was a staple in most meals; tamales or tortillas was also common. The kernels were boiled, ground down into a paste, then shaped by hand into flat tortillas before being cooked on an open griddle. Other crops they grew included beans, squash, pear, sweet potato, cocoa beans, vanilla beans, tomatoes, as well as a variety of fruits. All these items were rotated in their diet, as well as the occasional turkey or rabbit for meat. After the Spanish came, they introduced domesticated pigs to the Maya who began to develop their traditional recipes with pork.

The Maya were unique in the sense they did not domesticate large animals for their needs like other civilizations in the area did. They raised dogs, turkeys, and ducks for food, but they hunted deer, rabbits, and boar in the wild, as well as fished. They used every part of the animal for food, tools, or clothing and did not waste the animal out of respect. Animal skin was commonly used to make clothing. The clothing would be decorated with paint or embroidery in designs of other humans or of nature. There would be religious significance to these designs. In fact, it is said that the decorative designs for a woman's traditional attire would appear in their dreams. A woman's traditional attire included three pieces: the *huipil*, a long, sleeveless tunic; the *enredo*, a skirt that would wrap around to cover the lower half of the body; and the *quechquémitli*, a shoulder cape. Men also wore traditional tunics but with less decoration.

The society was broken into a class structure with four main classes. By rank, they were the nobility (Almehenob'), priesthood (Ah'kinob'), the commoners (Ah'chembal uinieol'), and the slaves (Pencat'ob'). At the top were nobles, with the King being the most powerful. The King's role was hereditary, so power was passed down to the son after the father's passing. The priests in the society were the next most powerful because they were the advisors to the king and performed the religious ceremonies. Artists, mathematicians, scribes, medicine men, and architects fell into this class. In order to have received education in their field of study, they would have to come from a noble family. The next level of people were the commoners. The majority of Maya society were farmers, so most people fell into this category. The lowest rung of social classes were the slaves who were prisoners captured during wars, or people who had broken the law and was being punished. They would be used for physical labor when it came time to construct roads or pyramids.

Archaeologists believe they have even found insight into the Maya standards of beauty, and it is quite unique. They considered crossed eyes and flat foreheads to be beautiful. To help their children become cross-eyed, mothers would tie boards to their children's heads and tie wax beads in front of their eyes to encourage them to look in that direction. Scars were considered marks of courage and attractiveness, and it was common for men and women to cut their skin to achieve the scarring design they wanted. The elites in the society would sharpen their teeth to a sharp point and make incrustations with jadeite or gold, a sign of beauty and wealth.

The dance was another ritual to Maya culture where lavish costumes would be prepared and ornaments such as staffs, rattles, live snakes, and spears would be used. The costumes would depict the forms of the divinities. By dressing and acting like a god, the Maya believed that the god's spirit would overtake them, and they would be able to communicate with the deity to ask for their prayers to be answered.

Maya folk medicine was based on a belief of health being a result of living peacefully in society and illness being a consequence of the gods for misbehavior. Medicine was only practiced by those who had received an extensive education. They were called *shamans* and were meant to act as a messenger between the physical and spiritual world. Another word archaeologists have found is *ah-men*, which means "disease throwers."

Archaeologists have found in Maya medical texts that herbal remedies were used according to the color of the original plant. They are as follows:

>Red: for rashes, blood disorders, burns

>Yellow: a disease of the liver and spleen (color of bile)

>Blue: natural sedatives

>White: avoided because it was seen as a signal of death

Common plants that are believed to have been used in medicine include but are not limited to chili peppers, cacao, agave, and tobacco. Animal parts from fish, insects, birds, and crocodiles could also be combined into an herbal recipe. Plants would also be rubbed onto the skin in the form of plaster to protect the body from bad spirits.

It is believed *shamans* would commonly use mind-altering substances such as "magic" mushrooms, peyote, tobacco, and other hallucinogens found in nature. These hallucinogens were believed to be a way of communicating with the gods to plead for health and to ask mercy for sins, in hopes that the gods would restore the balance in a person and bring back their health. If not able to provide a cure, these hallucinogens would at least be used to give pain relief. Self-brewed alcoholic concoctions would also be used. Maya pottery and carvings depict ritualistic enemas to ensure quick absorption of the substance.

Other common traditional cures involved prayer, offerings, and sweat baths. Similar to today's modern saunas, sweat bath chambers were made of stone walls and ceilings with an opening at the top for air to be expelled. The Maya believed the steam created in this environment was the perfect way for the body to expel impurities and restore the balance in a sick individual. Newly pregnant women would seek revitalization in a sauna, while the sick would hope to heal themselves. Even Maya rulers are believed to have frequently visited the sweat baths in their region because it left them feeling refreshed and able to think more clearly when making decisions for their people. In Piedras Negras, a city from the Classic Period whose structural remains are in Guatemala, archaeologists have discovered eight stone buildings that were used as sweat baths.

Maya medicine, like many other concepts of their society, was all about balance. For example, in medicine, it was a hot and cold balance. If someone had a "cold" disorder such as cramps or constipation, they would be treated with hot, spicy foods. If they had a "hot" disorder such as diarrhea, vomiting, or fever, they would be treated with cold plants or cold foods.

Evidence has also been found that the Maya *shamans* demonstrated surgical skills as well. They sutured open wounds with human hair and would reset bones. There have even been marks found that show they drilled into skulls with primitive drills. Dental surgeons would file teeth into shapes and insert decorative pieces made from gold, jade, turquoise, or other organic material. This was often done by the nobility as a sign of wealth and rank. Dental prostheses have also been found to assist those who may have lost teeth in battle.

Even today, male religious fraternities called *cofradias* have worked to preserve the steps and history of the traditional Maya dances. These men take their knowledge of the ancient dances as a very serious responsibility, researching and perfecting the dances and ensuring they will be passed to the next generation in the most authentic form they can. The Pop Wuj dance is done to show the four stages of creation that the Maya believe humans went through: the Man of Mud who did not praise the gods, the Man of Wood who was too rigid and was destroyed by the gods, the Monkey Man who was too silly and ultimately was also destroyed, and the Human Being, the current Maya, who prays to the gods to thank and praise them.

The Maya game Poc-a-Toc, which was technically a ballgame, had a much more religious significance than being just a pastime. Seven men would make up a team, and two teams would play on the ball court to gain points by scoring a rubber ball through a hoop on the far wall. Sometimes, the hoop would be as high as twenty feet, sometimes higher. They would also have to defend their own goal. The unique and impressive thing about it is that using hands and feet was against the rules: only their hips, head, knees, and shoulders were to be used. Diego de Landa, a Spanish bishop, wrote that watching the game being played was like watching "lightning" because the Maya players moved so quickly. Written records of how the game was played were destroyed by the Conquistadors, so researchers learned of it through oral history passed down the generations. It was previously believed that the team that lost would be killed at the completion of the match, but historians have analyzed glyphs and archaeological evidence to infer that even the winning team or captain could be killed to give them a quick path to heaven. Prisoners of war would be forced to play against the Maya in a reenactment of the war. The losers, the prisoners from a different city who could not play the game well, would be executed.

The game is symbolic of the Hero Twins' victory over the underworld lords, but it also hints at the Maya's cyclical belief of all things in nature. It is obvious from the human sacrifices that this was more than just an amusing game for Maya but a deep, spiritual part of their life and that the men who were chosen to play were honored by the society.

Chapter 12: Maya Technology

We have already spoken at length of how advanced the Maya numeral system was, as well as their knowledge of the number zero and how this led to their very accurate calculations regarding the astronomical lunar and solar cycle. Alongside this, it is also important to note the other advancements of this civilization.

For example, the elaborate temples and great cities that are still present to this day were all built without the essential modern tools of metal or the wheel. Other Mesoamerican civilizations used the wheel and found it extremely helpful, but the Maya did not use it because they did not domesticate animals like those other societies. Without animals to carry the cart, the Maya developed a different device called the tumpline, or *mecapal*. It allowed them to carry 125 pounds on their back comfortably. There was a strap connected to a frame to support heavy loads.

The Maya built their huge structures out of limestone, carefully crafted and built to withstand the worst of the weathering over centuries. The Maya arch, as it has become known, was a method they independently employed, achieving the look of the Classic Western arch. They did so without shaping the stone structures, however, as they could not do so without the proper tools. Despite the foundational problems of the arch, it is still an achievement for the Maya and a distinct feature in their style of architecture.

They did use some innovations in their arts such as looms for weaving cloth and creating an array of colorful, metallic paints from mica, a mineral that still has its use in technology and making pigment paints today. They were also adept at making tools out of jadeite stone. The Maya did not have access to iron ore—the only ore source in Mexico is over a thousand miles north of the ancient Maya Empire. Because of this, the Maya dedicated black jadeite for use in their tools. On a scale of 1 to 10 of mineral hardness (the maximum is 10 for a diamond), jadeite falls between a 6.5 and 7. It is harder than even steel or iron. It is believed these were the principal tools used by sculptors, wood carvers, and artisans alike, as archaeologists have found jadeite tools in various shapes such as chisels, axes, hoes to indicate their employment in multiple ways and professions. Green jadeite is most popular in jewelry, but black jadeite, when the aluminum in the compound is replaced by iron to produce an isomorph compound, shows great strength due to the prismatic crystals in the chemical makeup. It is believed now that the Maya sourced black jadeite from the tectonic plate in the Montagua Valley of Guatemala.

The interesting thing is that archaeologists did not find these tools in the royal tombs of the dead kings. It can be inferred from this that these tools were passed down from artisan families and were kept in the lineage because of how valuable they were for their crafts. The skills, along with the tools, would be passed down to a new generation of learners. Obsidian, a volcanic glass found in a ring of volcanoes along the Pacific coast, was also used for making even stronger blades for knives and swords meant for use in battle.

The Maya was also the first civilization in Mesoamerica to build the equivalent of modern roads. Called *sacbe*, these roads were built along their jungle environment to facilitate travel between their city-states. This would have been very necessary because trading with their neighboring states was very important to the local economy. The roads were paved, and the trees and leaves around them were cut to make it more comfortable for travelers. Traveling kings used these roads, as well as traders who traveled the city-states for commerce.

Another important innovation to note is that of rubber. It is commonly believed that the vulcanization of rubber with other materials came from Charles Goodyear in America in the 19th century. But now historians are giving the Maya credit for producing rubber products three thousand years before Goodyear even came up with the concept in the late 1800s. Researchers believe that the Maya may have stumbled upon this process accidentally, such as through a religious ritual where they may have used the rubber tree. Once they realized how strong the plant was, they used it in a variety of ways such as making water-resistant clothes, binding for their books and tablets, and making large rubber balls that were used in their traditional game of Poc-a-Toc.

Chapter 13:
Maya People Today

Today, there are descendants of the Maya people who occupy southern Mexico, northern Honduras, Guatemala, and Belize. They are a people fiercely protective of their heritage. They speak their native languages, wear traditional clothing, and practice their ancient religion. The term "Maya" is a broad term referring collectively to the descendants of the people of that region, but after centuries of migration, there are many distinct societies and populations of Maya people with their own cultures and traditions that mirror the equally distinct societies of their ancestors. The belief that the Maya simply vanished because their cities were found abandoned is untrue. There are nearly six million Maya today who perform and adhere to their ancient traditions, and they would find the idea that their culture has vanished as insulting.

Guatemala, southern Mexico, Belize, El Salvador, the Yucatán Peninsula, and western Honduras have numerous populations that adhere to the ancient Maya culture. These cultures are also immersed in Hispanicized Mestizo culture due to the Spanish colonization, but some sects continue to emulate a traditional way of life, even speaking the Mayan language as a primary language. Anthropologists identify the most prevalent Maya language today as "Yucatec Maya," but speakers refer to it as simply "Maya." Spanish is most commonly a second or first language due to the prevalence of Spanish culture in the region. Today, the Academia de Lenguas Mayas (the Guatemalan Academy of Maya Languages) exists and works to preserve the language of the

Maya in Guatemala in a world where ancient languages are on the verge of being lost.

Though the region was influenced strongly by Christianity due to the 16th century conquest and the spread of colonialism, there are still old ways that are observed with a mix of Catholicism and Mayan mysticism. On Cozumel Island, shrines to the ancient goddess Ix Chel and the Virgin Mary are both present, and they are seen as one divinity. The Daykeeper of a village still has the Maya role of interpreting the energy of a day. Mayan rituals are performed in caves and on the same terrain where their ancestors once practiced.

The most famous Maya on the global stage is Quiche Indian Rigoberta Menchu, the recipient of the 1992 Nobel Peace Prize for her work in social justice fighting for the rights of indigenous people. She is a well-known activist, fighting for the rights of the Maya people to practice their culture and region, as well as for feminist rights. Though there were some controversies that arose later regarding her recollections for her autobiography, the Nobel Committee dismissed calls to revoke her Nobel Peace Prize. She is also a UNESCO Goodwill Ambassador and has run for President of Guatemala in 2007 and 2011. Despite losing in the first round both times, in 2007, she gave a heartfelt message of peace on television for all Guatemalans.

Conclusion

Thank you for making it through to the end of *Maya Civilization*. Let's hope it was informative and able to provide you with a background of the ancient Maya civilization and the history of its people. We wanted to include information on the timeline of the Maya so that the growth of their civilization can be charted. They went from being a collection of small groups to being builders of huge temples and pyramids, growing nearly a dozen different types of plants to provide for their population. At one time, the biggest Maya cities could have been home to nearly 100,000 people. Considering these structures were built without modern tools or even the assistance of the wheel to carry stones, this was an impressive feat for the Maya, showcasing the intellectual capacity of the civilization.

Information on their cultural traditions had also been covered, as well as their religion, architecture, and their advanced knowledge in the fields of mathematics and astronomy. Despite being a Stone Age society, their calculations on the lunar and solar calendar were very close to today's calculations. Among many other things, we also learned about the Maya calendar and how they grouped together years to form a unique concept of time.

The next step is to dive deeper into Maya artifacts, visit their museums or ancient temples, and view their stone carvings that exist to this day. A trip to Central America to truly appreciate their ancient sites might be required, but it will surely be worth it. There are many museums open in the region that honor the Maya history, and descendants today can even perform traditional dances and sell their hand-crafted goods.

Finally, if you found this book useful in any way, a review on Amazon is always appreciated!

www.ingramcontent.com/pod-product-compliance
Lightning Source LLC
Chambersburg PA
CBHW052133110526
44591CB00012B/1709